WHAT MY FATHER NEVER TOLD ME

By

Tara Fox Hall

Author's Note: This novel is based on real life events. I have taken liberties with some names, and event dates have been changed slightly, to protect persons still living.

PROLOGUE

My father was the first to break my heart.

I always knew I wasn't good enough. If I had been good enough, he would have wanted to spend time with me. He would have wanted to help me discover the world, not shoot me down whenever I tried to fly. There would have been family vacations, and holidays that lasted longer than forty-five minutes before an argument ensued. He wouldn't have mistakenly called me by his girlfriend's name, or shown up drunk with terrified stray cats in Have-A-Heart Traps riding in the open bed of his work truck. He wouldn't have left messages singing songs about "Why To Be Nice To Crackheads" sung to the tune of Happy Birthday on Christmas Eve.

In life, we couldn't find a happy medium, and spent the last few years not speaking. An email from my aunt challenged my resolve in the time it took to read that my dad was having emergency surgery for the most aggressive form of brain cancer in existence. Globular Mastoma, stage four. Terminal, of course, even if he survived the surgery. If my dad had any kind of luck his whole life, it was bad luck.

Brain tumors aren't forgiving. Even with the mass gone—and a huge stitched up gash on the side of his head to prove it—my dad didn't make a lot of sense in his last few weeks. Inserted in the tumor site were chemo wafers, which caused him to switch randomly from topic to topic when conversing. Sometimes he was sweet, and sometimes he didn't make sense. There was only one night he seemed to be himself, the dad I remembered. The next day he stopped eating.

His end went fast, at least. The surgery only bought time. Once Dad understood that, and how limited his future options were, he opted to starve to death. Nothing my uncle or I said would make him reconsider, and he died the week after going off his medication in early spring.

He left behind a mess of unpaid bills, some with years of interest, and three houses in various stages ranging from hoarding to utter disaster. It was in his first house, the one I lived in briefly as a baby, that I found diaries that opened up a stark window to the man I never knew.

At first, I took only one diary, as a kind of way overdue payback. The reason I was there sorting through his piles of shit from the last forty years was to find my long-ago diary that he had taken when I was fifteen. Yet as I began to read the pages he'd filled, a singular story emerged from all the debauchery, self-pity, insecurity, and sadness. Here was a man I didn't know or remember, opening a window to his soul, showing me events from my own childhood circa eight years old from an utterly different point of view. Compelled, I returned to the house multiple times in search of more diaries, to try to unlock the secret of why my father had been the way he was.

CHAPTER 1: BACKGROUND

As I've said, Dad and I were estranged for a few years before he died. We'd had falling outs before, and sometimes not spoken for months. When I was younger, reconciliation happened because my mother told me to make up. When I was older, I either relented on his birthday to bring him cookies, or my aunt interceded to set up a get-together at her house for some abstract occasion. Either way, he and I always just began talking like nothing had happened. None of the recurring issues that repeatedly tore us apart ever got talked about, or solved.

I tried a few times to talk about deep issues, with no real result. I confronted him about being an alcoholic once. Concluding that snail mail was the least likely to pick a fight, I sent him some literature with a note to say I was worried about him, and that I'd support him to stop drinking. He never mentioned my packet, until I finally asked him point blank about it. He basically shrugged via phone and said, "yes, you're probably right, but I'm too old to change." After that, I gave up, deciding to accept him as he was with the rule of limiting our actual time together. Regular phone calls remained my way of staying in touch in the final speaking years of our relationship.

***

He'd sometimes show up at my home out of the blue with some unskilled worker he'd hired for minimum wage—usually trash, especially as he got older. This label might seem a harsh judgment; except for all the eventual tales I'd hear after he fired them for stealing from him, or crashing his truck, or ruining equipment. Most of the time he never got a chance to fire them, because they would just steal from him and disappear. Year after year, the names changed, but the stories stayed the same. In fact, part of the reason the second house—what was once my grandmother's house, a cozy if dated place I remembered with bittersweet nostalgia—was an utter disaster was because of these stellar people my father kept as part of his inner circle. He rented my grandparents house after he inherited it from my grandfather to a woman on welfare for easy money. She tore out the lathe walls, and used them for bonfires in the backyard. She sold drugs out of the house, leading to police visits, and an eventual neighborhood uprising against my father by the neighbors who had loved and respected my grandparents. They sent my father letters, and took the little legal action they could, to no real avail. Eventually, my father was able to evict her, but the house was unlivable by then. To compound that, my father tore out more walls, bragging about the dream house he was going to build for himself, Jacuzzi and bidet included. But he ran short of funds almost as soon as he retired, the same time his health took a nosedive. He picked trashy people to check on the house during the winter, and one of those people left the back door open, and the pipes froze and burst. His electric bill also went unpaid, and the power was shut off. The same saga of Repair Hell happened in his first house, 34 Mason St., with the same result. The difference is that that house had been his for decades longer, and the hoarding there was much more intense.

Dad and I never really got along well. I never really understood why. It seemed like we couldn't be in the same room for a few hours without some kind of argument unfolding, usually because sooner or later he would say something teasing to be funny that instead was either cruel or just nasty. I remember telling him once about my husband-to-be, how we had gone to a dinner party with his friends. His reply was that was good, at least Erik wasn't ashamed to have his friends meet me. I remember further back, being at one of the few overnight hot-air-balloon rallies with him, and one of his friends complimenting me after I was feeling self-conscious after being rejected by the handsome son of another friend. Dad's comment in a derogatory tone was, "You shouldn't say that, you don't know where she's been." Both times I was taken aback and hurt, wondering why in the hell he's say something like that. Everyone says things they regret, but dad's casual meanness was a particular habit, not a one-time event. I'd like to excuse it with some reason, like the cancer he was eventually diagnosed with was slow growing. But the truth is that attribute was just my father's cutting sense of humor. He thought he was entitled to treat his loved ones however he wanted to, and they were supposed to take it and love him anyway. His brothers still think that's a family policy to live by. I don't.

My husband Erik and my dad had a falling out one Christmas over my dad calling him "a selfish fuck," and my uncle took his side, and I felt compelled to take Erik's, as having seen my dad's behavior and being an occasional victim of it, I felt I couldn't subject Erik to him anymore after that. So we got uninvited for the following Christmas Day celebration and I didn't speak to any of them for years. I would often still drop off cookies on my father's birthday, and or send him a card. There was never any reply. I learned later for the last few years my father wasn't even living at the house on Mason St, so I've no idea if he knew I was thinking of him. In my searching after he died, I did find a book I sent him and a package of self addressed, postage-paid envelopes and stationary I had given him, to keep in touch. All were opened but unused, of course. They also must not have mattered to him, to have been left there after being opened.

In the first days after the surgery on his brain, my father was at first out of it, then argumentative and really shitty for a few days, to the point I considered just walking away again. He was in a wheelchair with oxygen, and pretty much refused to do everything. Initially he had told me to go to his old house and take anything I wanted, boasting of diamonds and cash he had hidden which I doubted was still there, if it had ever been. Days later he told me that I could not have anything, even my diary, the one thing I did want from that godforsaken house. He would not talk to me for hours, in spite of my efforts to get him to talk. I couldn't even convince him to sign the doctor's consent to treat him at the oncologist's office. To my relief, the nurse eventually convinced him to sign, and we were shown in to see the doctor.

The office visit would have been funny in its pointlessness, if it hadn't have been so horrific. A grim-faced doctor showed me a pages long report telling me with clinical distance what I already knew: the surgery had just delayed the inevitable and the cancer would be coming back to kill him. More horrible still, the doctor kept trying to ascertain if my father was listening to what was said, with no response. Finally, she turned to me and said, "Does he understand that its terminal? I have to make sure he understands that."

Overwhelmed, I grabbed the report from her and handed it to my father. "The cancer you have is terminal," I said harshly.

"There's nothing more they can do. If you understand that, say yes, or they aren't going to let us leave."

My father, who had not spoken a word until now, nodded and said yes. And then we were finally allowed to leave. As we checked out, I made several follow-up appointments, silently wondering what the point was as I made comforting mindless chatter to my dad.

As I drove him back to the nursing care facility, I made my plan. There was no way I wasn't getting that diary, whatever I had to do.

***

Furious, I got a key from my aunt and uncle that next week, and went to Mason, determined to find my diary. Even having seen the house was a hoarder's paradise for years, I was not prepared for the utter mess it had become. There were wall-to-wall boxes of stuff, and garbage on the floor, along with copious amounts of mail from at least two decades. There was no heat, no electricity, and no water: a burst pipe on the second floor had poured water into what had been the living room, and everything in there had a layer of mold and rot. There was still food in the downstairs refrigerator and mini-fridge upstairs from close to 2 years ago before. The bathtub was filled with empty food cans and dirty utensils, as was the downstairs sink. Everything not wet was covered with copious dust. I looked at that horrific scene all around me and thought, *Fuck it, I have to try.*

My father, in one of his lucid moments, had told me that my diary was in his bedroom. So I started there. It wasn't long before I began to find salvageable stuff I wanted to save: photos, cards I had sent him, my book I'd written and signed for him, old sheets of stamps, photos of my mom and me when I was little, and when he and mom were first married. I went out to my car, and came back with bags. Before I was there an hour I'd filled them.

I looked around at all the stuff still there: usable clothes, trinkets, frames, magazines, books, videos, blankets, and resolved to come back, with help. My father was about to lose his houses—all of them—for back taxes in a few months, whether he died or not, and all of this was going to get shoveled into a dumpster. I was not letting some stranger bin my memories. This was the only inheritance I was getting—there was no will, per dad's lawyer. And my father's paid-lover's sister had already tried to get him to sign a new will they had drawn up making them his sole heirs. I was getting my damn diary, one way or another.

**

    43 Mason always had an unsettling murmur of a house that was unhappy. Without my father's presence, abandoned and on the verge of being condemned, that murmur was magnified to a scream. A few hours were the longest I could spend there without depression settling in, even with others there to help me sort the detritus. I always felt as I searched that I was sifting back through the events of my life, as so many trinkets I found brought back memories. Hating to donate what I was enjoying remembering, I saved more than a few clothes and other salvageable items that I found as I searched, like the New Orleans T-shirts from our one solo trip together, and the sachets and neck warmers I'd made him over the years.

    As I've said, the front dining room was mold-ridden. I did salvage two unmatched sheepskin cushions, both of which washed just fine and are still in use in my car to date. Two others that were matched were too far gone, and made a huge mess in my washer when they disintegrated. I also found a four ounce Rolling Rock beer can filled to the top with pennies. I have no idea if my father put them in there or one of his cronies, only that the can was so packed full of pennies that I had to cut the can open with tinsnips to get them out. The endeavor had to take hours, in any case. The purpose eluded me. Boredom? A challenge to fit a certain number in?

    An "almost" room with a sliding glass door, a filing cabinet, and many large plants and plant hangers was also mold-ridden; the plant now long dead some thirty years, the earth in the pots like powder, the walls finished but never painted. Dad had decorated instead with visitor's ink, by having guests sign their name on the wall, or write their phone number or draw a picture. Soon what remained resembled crazy wallpaper, most of the writing illegible. Here I was able to retrieve my father's hot-air balloon pilot's license and various balloon documents from the cabinet and stacked boxes heaped with papers.

    The kitchen had many dishes, but with no water to wash the mouse droppings off them, I left most where they sat. Same with the food, as I didn't have extra money to buy special garbage bags to dispose of the trash and garbage; there was far too much, requiring a dumpster. Instead, I did what I could to save what was savable. My car was packed full each time I left with items to donate to the Salvation Army; there was no space left for garbage. I did take sensitive papers as I came across them, and all photos/videos, planning to destroy anything that I didn't want to keep. But I also took items that I gave to others that I thought could use them, from books to videos, shirts, trinkets, ashtrays, anything that I thought could be saved.

The front room was dedicated to tools, all of them broken. We made a path to the second floor, and left the rest.

The back room of the second floor was where my father threw all of the gifts he got or things he bought that he didn't want to use. At one point it had been an extra bedroom, with a filing cabinet in one corner, and a low dresser running the length of the back wall, a mirror running the length of the adjoining wall. I was saddened to sort that room, as I found most of the gifts I'd scrimped and saved to buy for dad over the years just tossed there to rot. The Predator-Friendly wool sweater I'd wanted so much for myself, but could only afford one for him on my part-time salary during my first years in college. Year's worth of high-quality cold weather socks, that he told me he needed each year and I always bought. A huge pack of black sharpies, for him to use in billing. The list went on and on. I began to feel as if it were just my gifts, until deep in the back I found a handmade stained glass box that my uncle had made for him, still in the original packaging with the heartfelt letter it had come with. Horrible as that was to find in the pile of discards, it made me feel not so alone, that it wasn't just my gifts that had been tossed in here to be forgotten.

This same back room was also where my father's first closet had been. Included with the regular clothes were some heavily elaborately embroidered shirts, and his work shirts. Thankfully, most everything was in dry cleaning plastic bags as he hated to do his own laundry, so paid to have everything dry cleaned. Emptying that and donating most to the Goodwill took the better part of two carloads. The additional adjoining backroom also held more clothes, broken glass, and water damaged magazines, my father's long forgotten book collection (circa 1970's 1980's), his matchbook collection, his porn, his balloon manuals, broken and old video equipment, and knickknacks of all kinds.

The middle room was the one bathroom in the house. It appeared to have doubled for my father's kitchen and closet in his last weeks there. Mice had infested the house, but signs were worst there. A pile of rotting towels and food lay on the unfinished floor near the toilet, the minibar was filled with oozing batteries and rank food, and the aforementioned bathtub was full. A portable heater, my father's only heat after his furnace died and he refused to replace it, was still plugged in. Like most of the machines my father had in his lifetime, it didn't work properly, even with my stepfather fine-tuning it. But it worked well enough for us to keep, for use in case of emergencies.

The front room to the left of the bedroom was filled with garage door parts, work paperwork, and camera paraphernalia. There was also a box of what looked like change, which I sorted out and kept. Change was one of my father's original hoarding triggers, and I found some in almost every room, like the aforementioned beer can. It was my father's tendency to scatter though, not sort, so the change was on the floor, mixed in in with other things in boxes, in drawers, and—my personal favorite—mixed in with old batteries leaking acid in an ashtray.

My father's bedroom contained a lot of garbage, stamps dating from 1977 to 2007, more pocket change in random places, tons of porn of all kinds, and all manner of scribblings. Strangely, there were some dollar bills folded carefully and intricately into a Band-Aid box, all ones. Also lots of clothes, including women's lingerie, in various sizes, some still unworn in packaging. This was where my father spent all his time, and where he kept what was most important to him. I was touched to see that included one bottom drawer where his deed to his house was kept were many cards that I had sent him over the years.

The attic was a squirrel domain of shredded paper knee deep, and contained older boxes from my father's life with my mom, his early life with his brothers, and more porn. The wreck was next to impossible to sort through, but I salvaged a lot of things like paintbrushes, Canadian coins, New Zealand currency from my father's trip to Antarctica, towels from his second marriage to my stepmother Rosette, sheets of hot air balloon stamps, comic books, writing pads, stationary, carved boxes, etc. Most things had been ruined by water or animals, but many were salvageable. One of those things was the infamous pennies.

Years ago, my father had kept a five gallon jar of pennies that he added to at the end of each day. One weekend, his girl and he were short of beer and needed cash. So they got all the pennies out, rolled them, and took the forty dollars worth to buy beer. Except no one would take the rolled pennies to buy the beer. So they got pissed off, she left, and my father took the rolled up pennies home and forgot about them.

I found the pennies in a box, corroded to the point they were green as they had been peed on for years by attic mice as the mice chewed on the wrappers and other nest material in the box. Apparently sitting and peeing on pennies is a mouse's choice of lavatory, because nowhere else in the house stunk as bad as that box. Beyond disgusting about sums it up. However to me, money is money. I carted the box home to my tub, separated the pennies from the remains of their wrappings, and scrubbed them with Lysol and detergent, then gave them a quick dry with a towel. The coin-sorting machine at the bank did the rest.

This anecdote sums up a key facet of my father: he would never do the smart thing when confronted by an obstacle, if doing so hurt his pride in the process. No one can refuse to sell someone of age beer for cash; it was his refusal to unroll the pennies that stopped them from trading them in. It was almost as if he couldn't admit he had wasted his time rolling them.

I admit I wasted time myself searching that disaster for my diary. In spite of my passionate vows, I never found it. I assume that it got put in a dumpster, and it now rotting in some landfill. I hope so, at least. I also never found the one other thing I wanted from Mason: a velveteen bag of lead crystals, most white, but some red or purple, all cut into many different faceted shapes. My father showed it to me years previous, when I was only eight or so. The crystals were unused inventory from when he owned and operated a small store out in the boonies. He let me have only one, and put the rest away, using them as he usually did as a bartering chip for my affection, saying I could have another when I came back to his house to visit him. He did give me another years later, but after that refused to give me more. They are also probably rotting in some landfill, or maybe someone is making a quick buck selling them on eBay. I'm happy not to know, either way.

Of all the things I didn't expect to find, my father's diaries top the list. Sure, finding my inpatient paperwork from my brief visit to the state hospital for depression as a teen casually left on top of the bathroom mini-fridge—reading material for the go?—was a shock. Finding naked pics of my stepmom and my father's paid-lover, the envelope of pot, and the packets of unmarked pills were less of a surprise. But my father had never told me he kept a diary, and didn't seem to be the kind of man that would pour his feelings out on paper on any kind of regular basis. Yet the more I looked at all the paper, the more I found poetry, fragments of crazy stories, letters that he never sent, and buried deep in hundred of pages, something of his fractured soul.

As I've said, I took the first diary as payback. But that's just the rationale. Initially, I saw the day planner from 1982 with the black leather cover, and just thought I'd flip through. I happened to open to a page where he seemed to be writing some kind of erotic story. Intrigued by the fairly decent writing—and wondering if I could use the idea/scene in one of my own books—I took the diary home to read.

* * *

It's taken me a year and a half to finally work up to writing this book. I've used almost every excuse to not work on it that I can. But I'm out of excuses and its time, even if I'm not ready. In some sense I think I might never be ready, because the source material is uncomfortable to read. A lot of what I found as I read—and I have now read through everything once—made me angry, depressed, sad, or all of these at once.

I fought with the idea of making the diaries part of a fiction story, to hide the worst bits under the quick save of "don't worry, that bit I wrote isn't real." I'm not writing this memoir to hurt anyone, or make people think ill of my father. If you personally liked whatever you knew him as, I'm not about to make you think otherwise. Just put this book down and give it away. But for those of you who want to see more of the man he was, thank you for reading.

As much as I didn't want to know some of what I do now, I wouldn't ever go back, and leave that diary there on the floor.

***

My last good memory of my father is the evening I saw him for an hour or so, and he was himself. It was good, that one night; I had got him some new clothes both some from his house that I'd wished for familiarity, and also some new superhero pajama pants. I read him a story of a hot air balloon flying cat, <u>Hot Air Henry</u>, that he had read me years ago. My mom had baked me a huge bag of chocolate chip peanut butter cookies, and I brought him that, too, as I didn't have time to bake. He ate one after the other, literally groaning about how good they were. We talked a bit, and joked, and laughed some, and told each other we loved one another when I said goodbye. That night I thought we'd turned some kind of corner, though looking back, I'm not sure why I thought that with surety. Maybe because I wanted an end to the stress of the last few weeks which didn't end with him dying.

It wasn't to be. The next day his "girlfriend" (in reality, his paid-lover) visited him with her sister. Both were pissed at not being left everything (as mentioned before, she and her sister had him sign a new will on a piece of notebook paper the eve before his surgery - his lawyer tossed it as invalid). There is no reliable record of what was said, but it must have been momentous. She never came back to visit him after that. After seeing her, he refused all medication, no matter what my uncle pleaded, and would not eat. He said nothing about why, or what had happened with his girlfriend (who denied she had said anything to him to make him refuse food and want to die). He quickly stopped making any rational sense as his brain swelled, and his organs began to fail. He died a week later, as the meds were the only thing keeping him from drowning with his COPD.

I'm glad that we had one good time after all the bad, but I'm not sure that it was worth a hundred thousand dollar surgery, or to have him go through all that suffering. Watching it, he was not having a good time, and as much as his suicide was hard to watch, the surgery only bought him a few weeks or months, at most. The experience makes me wish assisted suicide were legal. I do know if I get diagnosed with a terminal disease, I'm finding some way to end it before I go through what he did.

Now…onto the diaries.

CHAPTER 2: RUNNING DOWN A DREAM

The diaries aren't complete; most have gaps of days, weeks, or months. There are diaries from before my parents married and I graced the world, others from when I was in my late thirties. But the latter ones are almost incomprehensible, mostly a log of sexual escapades and expenditures for drugs, paid sex, and gifts for paid lovers.

The majority of the diaries are from when I was a few years old to when I was about twelve. I found none from my late teens, the months my father was in Antarctica, the ten years when he was living with my stepmother, or from the more than two decades when I was an adult, which included our trips to New Orleans and Florida. I'm guessing that some of these were lost through the years for various reasons, and also that he stopped writing for long periods for reasons of his own.

I'm not sure what I hope to find in sharing these pages. But it's clear that this time, writing's about coping with my pain and anger. A fictional character is not enough to channel it through this time, and it's going to take longer than a page poem to eradicate it. I will add that I spent more time with my dad in the summer after his death than I had in all the years previous. It's easier, when they're ashes.

***

After my father died, my aunt and uncle paid to have him cremated. They handled all the details, including unfortunately picking one of the most expensive places in town to have it done, a funeral home called Chase. The simple cremation, a cardboard "scattering container" with a setting sun on the front, plus getting to see his body in a room at the funeral home privately for a few minutes, cost a total of five-thousand dollars. I was thankful that they did this, as it was a thankless job; there was no inheritance to offset this cost. And I was still trying to cope of the shock of my father coming back into my life, having a terminal disease, and going through a "successful" surgery only to commit suicide. My mind at that time was badly scattered to the point that I lost my keys in the funeral home parking lot and spent an hour hunting for them, something that should have taken me all of five minutes, as the parking lot was almost empty.

My father died with a little over seven-hundred dollars in his bank account, which was only there as his social security check deposited after he died, so the two sisters he was living with had no way to get their hands on it. I claimed this as nearest living kin, and signed it over to the penny to my uncle. There were a bunch of creditors that were angry he had defaulted on various loans and credit cards, and with no will, they knew they were not getting paid. A few lawyer friends advised me not to try to claim either the houses or any monetary assets, because of this. However, my uncle was allowed to recoup up to the amount of the cost of my father's final expenses, by law. My uncle insisted on giving me a few hundred towards a trip I was taking as a "gift" which I gladly took.

After father was cremated, his remains were given to me by my aunt in that lovely, expensive sunset on the lake container from the funeral home enclosed in a cloth shopping bag from a paint store. I put him on the front passenger floor and left him there for weeks, as I wasn't sure I wanted him in the house. I had planned to scatter him, but now that I had him, I wasn't sure where to put him. My mom didn't want him at our cottage, and my husband didn't want him scattered at our house. I honestly didn't think he'd be happy either place, as he was the type of man who preferred to be with a lot of people. So, I carried him around in the front seat for a month. It was a nice time, actually, weird as this may seem. I told friends who were riding in my car that he was there; some were creeped out, others thought it funny when I introduced them. We went shopping (Dad stayed in the car), and I'd play him songs I knew he liked from his diaries, and from what I knew of him, like "Running Down a Dream".

Part of me was still angry about all of the things he'd done over the years and delighted to leave him in the car in a sort of limbo, as if to punish him. The other part just liked this chance to spend a little time talking to him when he couldn't answer back with some smart-ass comment, or not pay attention to what I said. Finally, I made the decision to scatter him at the end of the summer at a wilderness area in a local park, a site which was home to many festivals, including hot air balloon events.

I did have to go up to the family cottage by myself that same spring. Because I was depressed, I brought dad with me. I set the container on the porch so he could see the sunrise/sunset on the lakeshore. He seemed to like it, or so I told myself, so I left him there all summer. It was good to say hi to him as I had to my grandparents whose ashes were also scattered there many years ago. Mom also took delight in saying a few things to him while he couldn't say anything back that summer, when we read his diaries together. Our lake neighbors also got introduced, as they came over to visit. Sometimes we would laugh so hard, talking about him and the things he did, and I think he enjoyed that, to be the center of the conversation for his many exploits, some of them infamous.

It was on the last day that I took him shopping that I wrote the above passage, as I prepared to let go and spread his ashes. I think he liked where I chose to scatter his ashes. A park where he'll never be alone, even in winter. I played him Petty's "Running Down a Dream" one last time. I never liked that song myself, but knowing the lyrics, I see why my dad did. He was always in pursuit of the next good thing, so much so that he couldn't hold fast to the good things he already had. Too many of us make that same mistake, and like him, we don't usually see it. You might say that's first on the list of things my father never told me, but which I learned from him all the same.

***

The first diary I can find comes from January 1965. My father must be 21 years old. He has already met my mother, and sometimes is taking her back and forth to college in Cortland where she's living on campus, studying to be a teacher; she is either nineteen or twenty. His printing is clear and well spaced, easy to understand.

His first entry reads thus: "Charlie's New Years Eve party with Chris (my mother) at <his> parent's house in Chenango Bridge. Got Butch and Gail at 3. I fell asleep, took Chris home at 4, and came back. Left at 6 forcibly."

My mother always said that my father partied a lot, and that he never wanted to leave. That seems to be true, as this diary is on a calendar, with short entries on the days. On nights he stayed home and usually either watched TV, read Sax Rohmer's <u>Fu Manchu</u>, or studied/worked on something called an ICS (International Correspondence Schools?) exam, he writes it explicitly, then underlines it with red, a different color from the entry. My first thought is that staying home bothers him, as if it's boring, and he resents it, even as he is sometimes phoning my mom or writing her letters. It's also obvious from these entries that he's fooling around with my mom's sister Melanie, as one entry says they're kissing, and another they're making out. Melanie, or Mel, as she preferred, died when I was only a few years old of Hodgkin's disease in her late twenties. I never got to know her.

There are also other girls who he's dating as well. These girls are sixteen or so at the time—five years younger than he is. He doesn't seem to like them as people: one entry says, "Mel called to give me advice-Ha." He also does seem to be into my mother, noting their first dance, then one entry from 1/22 saying, "Tavern with Chris, Shield cut her down, I did nothing, broke down in car and told her I loved her." But noted under that on the same day is "Jewel, Park Diner, got in at four." I have to guess he took my mother home, then went out again later that same night. (Jewel or Jewelly I believe stands for Jules or Julian, a friend of my father who became obsessed with my mother and eventually killed himself). Apparently, this didn't go unnoticed, as on 1/27 the entry reads, "Barb squeal to Chris, I clam up, take girls home." The next day there is the note that he has "nothing to say to Chris when she calls." Yet the day after he apparently "explained to Chris about Mel (her sister)" and also Barbara, the one who alerted my mother who must also have been kissing him.

The next month is mostly bare, but the writing changes from printing to cursive with no explanation. Perhaps it was because he read <u>Lord of the Flies</u>, which he sums up as "good book-symbolic." March is the same, except for a notation that he's getting an army physical on the 30th. He is not drafted though, as his eyesight is too bad to be eligible for the service, though he did get dog tags.

April is again full, mostly from different parties (he's still hanging out with Jewelly when mom's away), working on the ICS test, and making out with unknown girls. He did manage to finish the ICS test on 4-4, and also quit smoking temporarily. But work is slow (he is working with my grandfather for Overhead Door in an apprenticeship; my grandfather wanted at least one of his four sons to follow in his footsteps as an overhead door repairman). But with 2 days in a row off due to slow work, my grandmother suggests that my father get another job. But he's also calling Barbara again, and going out most every night.

It's not 'til mid-May where I actually get another emotion listed, this one of anxiety. It's hard to say what happened exactly, only that it involved my father, the police, and a surfboard. He says his stomach is in knots, that a judge says he's skating on thin ice, and that he goes to the police station to get the surfboard back. Not sure what's going on, but he's out at all hours with all kinds of people, from a guy who steals him hot sausage to his regular friends and many, many girls. He's also anxious about my mother finding out about these other girls, as he is very relieved when he gets another letter from her at college. He also seems to be running through money, a lot of which is going to pay a florist and put gas in his older model used Jaguar, while he's only getting paid about $65-70 a week (Dad was famous for owning very fancy used cars that were on their last legs when he purchased them, and either never ran or only for a short time). He's also suffering from no sleep as he's out all the time, and my grandfather is getting "bitchy." So he does his first listed experiment with drugs in the form of No Doz, which he says "works good-good."

By June he's again trying to quit smoking but still doing No Doz. He's still getting bitched at by my grandfather, and wants another job. He's also still living at home with my grandparents, and my mom is still pissed off about him hanging with Jewelly. July is much the same, except here is the first mention of my stepmother Rosette, who must be about eleven or twelve at the time. August is blank except for the first four days, on which the notable thing is he finally finished the ICS course and sent it in, and that he got cited for urinating in public. September is also mostly blank, except for a note that says, "Chris told Jew(el) I guess." Told him what, I can't say.

The beginning of October is blank, but on the nineteenth, it's more of the same, except things seem to be coming to a head. My father is running out of money, even though his pay has gone up a few dollars. His car is not working and he's still wanting another job. He has some kind of fight with my mom on the 23rd when he goes to visit her at her dorm, as he gives her the finger, then from there its garbled: "park bad-blow it twice, disappoint, can't trust, feel terrible, idiot, talk of suicide, leave for home, kill rabbit." I suspect he is referencing a conversation with Jewelly and he's not sure how to handle his friend's depression. But then the next entry doesn't mention this at all, and goes back to listing people and parties and when he got home and how he got paid.

It's there that I begin to feel that same wrongness in the diary, that this is more a listing of what happened then a real diary, as there are so little emotions listed. There's not even a mark for his birthday, much less an entry, which is this month. It's almost as if he was too busy to feel anything for anyone in particular, and does not want to be bogged down by real emotions. He lists, "Weighty thoughts: Don't learn to laugh from a teacher who cries."

November is also blank, except for the week of the eighth. This is my first entry where I see one of his friends, someone named Harold. He asked my father for a loan. Three hundred and eighty-four dollars was all my father had in the bank, but after agonizing and avoiding the guy for two days, he lent it to him.

December is the first entry where I see my father's sense of humor not taken well. He has some kind of fight because of a gross card he sent (there are no names listed). There's also some kind of accident with my mother that gets the police involved, when a truck ran a red light. Later in the month there is also evidence of my grandfather's alcoholism, as my father writes he's asleep on the table, passed out. There were several mentions previously that my grandfather came home drunk, or was drunk, but this is the first one where he passed out. My father's also still trying to see Jewel and Melanie, my young aunt, is still pursuing him. But he does get $250 of the money back from Harold, at least.

Aside from the obvious cheating, this diary seems the most normal (aside from the public urinating, anyway).

***

The next diary is from December 31st, 1964- February 28, 1965. The rest of this year is missing, as is 1966 in its entirely. This one is on yellow lined paper, the kind that comes in a pad. Besides calendars and day planners, these yellow pads were my father's favorite diary medium. This diary begins on New Year's Eve 1964, where Jewelly arrives totally smashed [at my father's home. My father is having a party, but Jewelly is five hours early. They go looking for someone named Ron, but go to the wrong house. Jewelly is acting crazy, banging on walls, screaming, and scratching my father in the face. Finally, they find a few more people, including a friend called Nick whose car stalls and had to be picked up by a wrecker complete with police. My father for some reason enjoys this immensely, that it was a "great scene," that he "loved it." They all go back to my father's house and he plays host. Apparently, a lot of people end up throwing up and/or passing out, including Mel, my mom's sister. Jewelly (who grabs/gropes my mom before tossing his cookies in the bathtub), a few other women, and my father, who passes out afterwards. My uncle Dave ends up taking my mother home the next morning. "Some party," writes my father in closing.

The pages that follow are more of the previous year: my mother fights with him because of his other women, he's still messing around with my aunt Mel, and he's still going out to all hours. My grandfather is getting pissed at both my father and mother, and takes it out on my mother, telling her that she should "just get married and forget college." My father calls him a "sarcastic bastard," but of course not to his face. Dad also seems to be angry that mom's not "putting out." He's also trying to cheer up Jewelly, making him a card that says, "Happy Birthday! You may not be a prick, but you're no fucking angel" and another card saying "Birthday Greetings – Just to say you're not such a big prick after all." And he's reading *The Collector* at night. His writing is also beginning to get more elaborate, beginning first by using a symbol that looks more like a J than an I.

There is some big scene on 1-15, where my mother meets my father at their favorite bar The Tavern (a long ago place long demolished, existing now only in my fictional Promise Me Series as a hangout for Lash, Taken in the Night, Book 3). There they finally have a big fight about his other women. He tries to talk to her, but she ignores him, then finally cries. He loads her into his car with protest, then after more arguing gives her an ultimatum that if she leaves "that's it." He takes her home, but there's no ruminating about the fight. He goes right back to the Tavern and watches a cake fight between Jewelly and Dick, another close friend. En masse, they all decide to go to another bar, and play on the highway passing each other, having Chinese fire drills at all the red lights when they get to town. My father comes into the bar and announces, "Here I am, girls." A woman says hi, and he tells her "C'mere, Babe, it's your lucky night". He then leaves that bar with Jewelly, and after some more hijinks, another friend runs off the road, plowing the front of the vehicle three feet into the guardrail," but he's "not hurt too bad." Someone calls the police, and they follow the group to someone else's house, where the boy's father is waiting. He tells them to leave, and then "go down by the river to get their story straight." They chase a cat and decide to eat breakfast, but the one friend who didn't crash is still racing them to the restaurant. They get their story straight over breakfast "terrible French fries and gravy," then my father goes back to drop everyone off at the Tavern. He doesn't get home until 5:15 in the morning.

The next day my father writes that he makes up with my mother, that everything "is okay again. I hadn't any hope for a while there." For not having any hope, he sure found ways to amuse himself.

1-17 is apparently my grandparent's anniversary; I had no idea. My father doesn't know what to buy them, and he's pissed at his father for not getting some operator linkage up and running: "That figures." My father finishes *The Collector*; "a sad and sinister story, I felt sorry for them both."

1-18 my father writes he went out that night with a girl called Amber (mentioned previously in the 1965 diary). "She wanted to kiss me, or at least she waited-I touched her lips-she said 'it's not hard to have a good time with you.'" And finally with this entry I admit to wanting to slap some sense into this man for being an idiot to my mother. I feel sorry for them both, him for being stupid about most everything, and my mother for wasting her time with him, and crying over him.

1-19, my father's first erotic dream listed, he writes that he's "making love" to another flame, Ann Marie, but that "she had a male organ, too." There's not any notation about just how fucking weird this dream is, he just goes right on: "great day at work, and heard two songs I want, "Wonderful Song", and "Love is Something if you Give it Away."

1-20, notable last paragraph, in that my father argued with his father because he wouldn't give his brother Dave a ride "cause I saw it as a favor for Dave and not mom, and I was busy. They celebrated anniversary tonight. I decided not to give them gift as it would seem like I was bowing to them." What an ass.

1-21 <u>Last Exit to Brooklyn</u> is "a disgusting book, maybe because it tells of life-the real and sordid part in which everyone participates." He goes on to say, "I'm kind of depressed at Tavern, maybe because it's too much like the same old thing all the time." He goes on to add one of his women friends "kissed me upon entering," and that he was "affectionate to Chris most of the night, a fact which I'm sure she appreciated for a change." Duh, your life IS the same old thing over and over, except the stakes are getting higher, and the consequences more severe. And Dad, you're blowing it with mom and writing this diary like you're some great Don Juan. Sigh.

1-22 Mom decides to make dad jealous by flirting with Jewelly. Dad appears to be turned on by it, oddly, and they make out in his car for hours. He also writes that two friends got married today but he wasn't invited to either, "but that doesn't hurt my feelings at all." I can tell just by how this statement is written centered on the page and separate that it surely did just that.

Nothing notable until 1-26, when my father composes a song for his friend Dick:

> To a sailor it's a whore, whore, whore
> To a doorman it's a door, door, door,
> To Hugh Hefner it's a great big tit,
> To an Epileptic it's a fit.
> To a little kid it's a bike, bike, bike
> To Mike Q. it's a transit strike
> To a circus it's a tent, tent, tent
> To Dick its getting bent.
> Get bent, Birthday Boy!

I wonder if its genetic, if I have a predisposition to write erotica. And if this is where my weird erotic dreams sometimes come from.

1-27, my father sells his car, which has been giving him trouble consistently. The "Tavern is feeling melancholy again…Tomorrow is the big day, mixed feelings. Also, I think I'll buy skis." Separately is written in caps, printed, "Goodbye car, You've been great to me, Goodbye."

1-28, Dad buys Hunter's car, a Plymouth, Barracuda he's mentioned several times before, and shows it off until 3:30 at the Tavern, his notes filling up the better part of two pages with how much all his friends like it. Mom is sick, and he's tired of dealing with her father, who is "a bitch again," so he leaves her home and goes out, kissing some girl named Maureen. There's also "Lesson from Hunter: Buy and sell, buy and sell, hustle, always talk to people. Get something cheap that won't depreciate and hang onto it until you can sell it for profit." This is likely the impetus that begins my father's hoarding of basically anything collectible.

1-31, There's a huge snowstorm, "worse snowstorm my father can remember since moving here, "a foot and a half in three days and more coming." Dad, who to this point has not let any kind of snowstorm or zero degree temps keep him from going out all night, stays in and works again on his ICS course. He also has a talk with Mom. "I take you for granted," he tells her, "She's shocked— later I told her that she hurts me sometimes—real weird talk." She said, "I place too much emphasis on coolness. Maybe I do. Sometimes I don't get across what I'm trying to say from lack of concentration." What was your first fucking clue there, Dad? And how is it possible for someone to be so pathologically self-absorbed?

2-1, Mom and Dad have another talk, where she says he's changed and more distant. "She's grown accustomed to my flirting and other girls and so on." Pretty disgusting Dad, to be congratulating her on that, or that you'd think it was a good thing for her to get used to in the first place. Or that you went back to the Tavern to make out with Maureen, where you "try but don't push." Yuck!

2-3, My uncle Dave loses a school wresting match, "every time parents come, it seems" while Dad has yet another fight with mom. She calls him bitchy, they go out, he "kissed her though my thoughts were elsewhere, on other girls." Dad, how is there anything redeeming at all about what you're doing? How can you write as if you're proud of what you're doing, when it's disgusting?

2-4, more Dad being an ass, "Chris-sorely tempted to cut her down, she kept grabbing my hand." He's also bracing for a fight with his father, who wants him to work more and party less.

2-5, Dad remarks "I also like Chris better than anyone. Maureen is just a passing fad. I want to make out with everyone." That last is certainly the truth.

There is more sporadic nastiness to mom until 2-8, where my father finally learns how much money he is making working with his father: $2.20/hr. He works 46 hours that week, so gets a check for $82.49, after mandatory allocations to state and taxes. Here also Jewelly says he's suspicious of mom, that she's a 21-yr old virgin is "just a big act. Can't believe in a twenty-one-year-old virgin." Not sorry you killed yourself, asshole.

I think its possible they did have sex 2-12, at least my father remarks about some time with her at "the pumphouse," that is was the "best ever, even though it wasn't anywhere near the length. Saw trees through the window as if there was no glass. Chris said she is leaving in January, marriage is the balance. She says she's sorry if she pushed me into a corner. I tell her my plans-next Dec. ring and date." My father goes on to praise my mother's friend Ann Marie (who he's referred to as 'a hog' pages earlier) for talking to Mom, telling her "not to chase him or come home so often." Ah, the idiocy of women, to think they, by their own actions, can change anything a man is predisposed to do.

2-13 is the first mention of drugs besides No Doz. Of course, it's an aphrodisiac called Spanish Fly. I hope if he really did get seven pounds, he broke it up over several women, as the stuff was supposed to be very dangerous. (Mom, I hope you didn't take any). He quotes a friend as being "Hornier than a bucket of catfish," and misspells horny with an extra e, twice. He also sets the date for the wedding as 11-11-67.

2-14 is Valentine's day, and he sends his bride to be flowers, then states, "women think with their heart not their head." He should have written men like him think with their dick, not their brain. He also thinks about how my mom would "make a good wife, my freedom is the only hold back. I'll make the next two years count." My mom is besotted and thinks that he's come around, sending him a telegram, "I love you, let's get engaged soon." This does not set well with Dad: "she wants to get engaged now and change the marriage date. You would have thought she'd be satisfied, but it only added fuel to the fire." He then writes her this letter:

*Dear Christopher (*Christopher was my father's nickname for my mother), *I'm not sure you're going to like what I'm going to say at all, but my minds made up and that's how it will stay.*

This weekend you gave me an ultimatum, a choice, call it what you will. In any case, I made the choice, and I must admit that part of it was easy. The next thing you wanted was something definite. I told you definitely the time of our engagement and forthcoming marriage. Now you can't wait to get married and want to change the marriage date. Now one concession leads to another, and if you had your way we would be married in the next six months. This is sheer nonsense, and one of the reasons I neglected to tell you of all my plans, or set a definite date before this. You are jumping into this with your heart and not your mind and I refuse to go along with it. My plans still stand. Love, Douglas.

All the irritation I have felt for my father 'til now comes to a head with this bullshit excuse for a letter. I want to look back through the years and tell my mom, run, leave this bastard and never look back, because he doesn't love you. He doesn't care about anything but himself, and he's never going to change. Here's the perfect excuse to find your balls. Tell him what for, and get him out of your life. Anyone that loved you would want to marry you, would be ecstatic you wanted him as your one and only, and would get engaged now, even if they wanted to stick to the agreed-on date. And no one but a total shit would give this letter to someone on Valentine's Day, either. Just why you want him so much and went on to marry him, I don't understand.

There's a footnote in the next page that states my mother changed her mind, and will go along with my father's plan. He's too busy though preparing for a court date over some issue, he pleads not guilty 2-21, and posted bail, with a hearing set for April. My grandfather says "For God's sake don't get another one before your trial date," which makes me believe its some kind of vehicle violation, either speeding or driving drunk. The next day Dad drives up to see mom. They look at diamonds, but by the next night he's trying to puzzle out his current "problem-how to make out with both Maureen and Mel." He ends up choosing Maureen.

2-24, he discovers Verve, which he says "works longer and better than No-Doz." I looked online to find what this drug was, as I'd never heard of it. Verve is apparently another name for GBH, a drug similar to ecstasy.

2-25, he's out with Dick and Nick, they had been thrown out of several bars, Nick got a ticket for 60 in a 30mph zone, and they still want to go to a bar that's open 'til 3. My father "goes along for the ride." Nick goes to sleep in my father's lap, and they kill a rabbit with their car, as the roads are icy and it's snowing. He drives them to a bar, they get turned away, he drives them to another bar, falls asleep in the car, then awakens when they get back in. Jewelly must meet them there, because he drives off with them and "goes up a side street" (after Nick gets through with his car) and "rams a snowbank, his car gets stuck, and the battery fails." They take the still-mobile car and leave my father there with no keys looking for help, and he "drinks a beer to keep warm." His friends come back with the police but somehow no DWI/DUI, and a large tow truck has to finally get the car out. They pay the tow truck driver nine dollars and twenty-seven cents for the help, and then jump the dead battery. Jewelly is "more smashed if possible, and still driving. I went to sleep ½ the way home. Nick took me back to Tavern" (to get car) and they witness Jewelly spin out. Dad finally gets home at 5:30 in the morning. He's out of it the next day, but that night he's back in the Tavern for hours, not getting home until 2 am. The next night is the same.

I don't understand why a person would want to go out night after night, watch their friends get drunk and puke, drive in the dark on bad roads to kill animals and nearly get killed yourself. This makes interesting fictional reading, yes, but how can you really live like this? This kind of out of control power drinking and resulting vehicular menace is why mothers formed M.A.D.D in the first place, and it's amazing that no one was killed. This behavior is pathological and somewhat sad, because this craziness is what some people go through the first month they can drink legally, then they grow out of it because doing that night after night becomes boring very fast. My father seems to never have grown out of this phase. Worse, it seems he never wanted to. What an unbelievably pointless and sad existence. And Dad, FYI, it's not cool at all.

1966 is missing, so fast forward to 1967. This year, at least, my father seems to have kept his diary writing a bit more regularly. I took a few days off to think about these entries, and am trying to go into this next year with the attitude that here at that time in history, the culture is much different on what is acceptable behavior over fifty years later, and Dad was only 21 years old. Kids do things that don't make sense to their parents, and think it's normal, because it makes sense to them. Grown people want everything to make sense. Immature and mature are two perspectives that look at life from opposite sides, something my parents were about to discover firsthand.

***

January 1967 seems to have begun momentously. On New Year's Day, Dad says he and mom "brought in the new year right this morning. The next day he begins "abstinence" and also a beard. On the third, he gives mom her engagement ring. He seems to be trying hard to be good this month, staying home about half the time, going to dinner with my grandparents, and spending time with mom. He gives up on his beard on the fifteenth, and shaves it. But by the nineteenth, he's back to his real self, or maybe just left that off his earlier calendar entries. In any case, he admits to my mother that he went out with some woman named Linda, and "Told C I felt bad, <but> didn't really." On the 23rd, he loses his license (there are frequent mentions of cops, but with no notations that say ticket, just "ok" or nothing). On 26th, "Dick's birthday ended in a free-for-all brawl, me too, I brought cake."

February is mostly blank, except Dad sent mom flowers on Valentine's Day, he's studying ICS courses again, my grandmother is refusing to pack his lunches (?). On the 24th, he says "pissed at Chris," then he gets drunk by 7:30pm on Saturday, and misses picking up my mother by three hours. He apparently doesn't come home. Mom gets pissed off and goes back to school on Sunday by herself. Mom begins bitching at Dad a bit more in March, telling him, "my friends mean more?" I take the question mark means that Dad is somehow surprised she thinks this. He patches things up with her that following weekend, then spends the rest of the month partying and being tired from no sleep, including trying marijuana for the first time on the 14th. Dick and Joe go into the Army a few days later.

In April he is working every day between five and a half and twelve and a half hours, but there's also a lot of "Cold Duck" listed, and "gang bang" on the 23rd where there's a woman's name listed and the names of 4 specific guys, so maybe it was real.

May, Dad's beginning to like drugs as much as alcohol. He writes "really high" or "got smacked" more days than not, and unless he's using "acid" for his garage door repair work, then he's getting that drug too, for his own imbibing. That may explain the entry, "slow motion weight on back of head, laugh laugh, little kid again, very forgetful, paranoid, sense of time, distance, tired."

June of '67 is my mother's last days of being a student, as she prepares to step into the world as a young schoolteacher. As for Dad, he is still working a lot, learning to drive a dumptruck, and my grandfather orders a curfew for him.

July, my father writes, "bad news week, 14th-23rd, everything wrong, depression." That seems to be the truth, mainly because my mother gives my father a taste of his own BS, as she is hanging out with Scrub, a man with a crush on her that she likes, too. He writes, "told Chris no more Scrub or never-ring back. She wants him to like her so she can choose. She likes him a lot. Crush. Tell her my side. I'll wait." He loses ninety dollars playing cards, and then mom gives him his ring back on the 17th. "Everyone's laid off" on the 21st, "no pay." Mom and he seem to still be talking, "<she admits to him that she > made out with Scrub," and another guy, "Lynn, gave her a proposition. Made me feel real bad." Yet they make up again, and he cancels his date with Barbie G. to date mom on the 30th. Previous to this Dad has mentioned other guys flirting with mom or grabbing her, but with no jealously. Here finally there are the first stirrings of what in time became a full-blown obsession.

August seems full, every day filled completely. Lots of parties, almost fights, and drinking to the point of "smashed/smacked." On the 19th, Dad goes "up home to find parents drunk unbelievably, barf 2x at C's on whiskey sours." Not sure if these are her parents or his. Dad has an apartment now, and some nights he doesn't make it home, others people stay over at his place because of partying too hard. I also confirm this month a suspicion that my father's been marking days he has sex with mom with little female symbols. I noticed these a few months before, but there were no notes to confirm my suspicions, until this month. My mom also gives my father an onyx ring 8/4, to mark one such occasion. And he helps a little bird, something I find cheering without knowing any details, just because it is the very first entry where he mentions an animal he is assisting, instead of those rabbits he's always killing while driving drunk.

September is also full, to the point there is writing all over the margins of the calendar. It's hard to read, and I see where I get my inclination to do the same thing when writing out notes to stories. I resolve to try harder not to do that anymore; lines are there for a reason. But the month overall is good, my parents seem to be getting along, my father's eager again to get married, and is working hard to get money to pay his bills. This is also the beginning of his working insane days, as he describes 9-9, a fifteen hour day, as "one of my best days."

October is the same, mostly good, including my dad's birthday, which he says is "the best." He also gets contacts, which I didn't think were even available back then. He likes them, after a period of adjustment. He also worries about his own job when a friend is laid off, and puts in applications to go into another line of work. Somewhere here he also moves out of his parent's home and gets his own apartment.

November brings a great many changes. Dad begins a new job at Grandway, an electronics store, on the 2nd, where he says," its great to work in a suit-snow looks better when I don't have to work in it." He "sells 3 things. I've got a great deal to learn." He also has some issue with "LSD" and "cops" on the third. He sells more than twelve hundred dollars that first week, but only gets paid thirty-two dollars making him depressed, "but I'm happy, as I need the money." He is working most of the time by himself 10am-10pm, and he's not happy, being alone, even when he is selling, which isn't much. When a new guy Dave starts on the 22nd, he's "a pain in the ass <who> doesn't know dick," and "screws me out of sales." He's sick the rest of the week, but still okay enough to party and drink. He's also selling better as its close to Christmas, making seventy-two dollars that week, then eighty-nine dollars the next.

December seems to be a turning point. Dad now likes Dave, says he's "really helping him out" and gave him a TV "put your initials on it." My mom's "a lady." He says he's "never had more on my mind then now- bosses, new job and responsibilities to them and myself, to keep apartment or not, cleaning and eating, bills, Chris, Larry (his roommate, apparently), Harpur's, Chris (impending marriage and responsibilities), car and clothes, Anita ('hope to keep friend and no more'), bugs in bathroom." He's not selling a lot at the beginning of the month, but is paid on 12-7, so he "can eat." Anita is apparently after Dad, and "bothers" mom, who seems to be getting drunk herself some and barfing and passing out. He says he's busy and will get a good paycheck the following week, then the next week there's no pay, because something happened at Grandway where he had to "spend morning putting store back together…no pay. When we got busy at night I was back in stock room." A weird ending to the year, as there is nothing noted for Christmas, New Year's, or the rest of the month. Its then it occurs to me that I seemed to have missed my mom's wedding to my father. So I go back to November, and there's a notation with an arrow pointing to 11-11-67, "Chris and I would have been married today." Evidently the wedding is postponed.

This calendar is markedly different from the previous year of simple partying. While Dad is still going out with friends and having a good time most nights he's not working, having to take care of his living space and fix his own meals, plus doing his laundry is wearing on him. I know this feeling from my own transition to my own home many years ago, going from being taken care of to taking care of yourself. There is a lot less energy for fun and friends when bills have to be paid, and the house is a mess and you have to clean it, and life isn't going the way you thought it would. But there's also an awareness of responsibility that shows itself in the brief entries, in that Dad seems like he's trying to do what he knows he should.

There is a last writing on the cover, dated 11-15-17, but it's not an entry. This is the first poem of my father, a beautiful creation I'd think would be called, "Cold Moon."

It's a cold moon shining down
on a cold world tonight
The snow on the roof across the way

makes me more aware of my warm bed
The friendly sound of the
record player reproducing "Country Gold"
I'm alone, but I'm melancholy happy
It's a beautiful scene-I'll bet its chilly
out there
head resting on my hand
I write by the light of the moon
cold silvery moon

I'm sure he wrote "classical" poems before this, in fact, I know he did, as I saw some long ago in a scrapbook my mom had that was falling apart, which contained pages of little florist cards from flowers my father had sent her with loving words, some with poetry they both liked, such as "she walks in beauty like the night," others he penned himself.

My father had a gift for writing, and some of his works are beautiful, like this, others crude, like the birthday ditty previously mentioned, or humorous. I find this a reminder of his humanity, as in these poems, as well as a few choice passages to come later, I get a glimpse into the person he seemed afraid to really show in all his many notations of events and people….himself.

***

There is another calendar for 1968, but this is oddly only used through February, all the following months blank, except for one entry.

January is sporadic with entries, mostly selling little at Grandway, drinking, the undeterred Anita still after my father, and mom still jealous. February is the same, with my father "explaining to C how much I did for her-not to listen to parents, friends, Amy, Mel." He gets both her and Anita flowers for Valentine's day, and "C hurt-mad." That he could be so callous to his bride-to-be makes me shake my head. On the 18th, he and mom have some big "cry together" and talk and have sex, and "engaged 20 min ago. I think maybe time was wasted on Anita." It's hard to feel sorry for him two days later, when he gets laid off from Grandway, but I manage to, as he sold lots the previous week, and doesn't seem to get any commission or pay for that at all, at least there is none noted. Mom has called off the marriage, "talked out temp<orarily>, not sure if I'm happy or not- I really love her." He claims unemployment, and looks for other jobs, but nothing is listed. March is blank except for 21st, which says "Ann Marie, long time glittering eyes, I wonder?" I can well imagine what he's wondering. Sigh.

1970 is also missing. 1971 is too, but I have a letter from my uncle David to my father that's dated that year. This book may be about my father's writings, but I include this letter, as it shows yet another POV I was never privy to.

> *Douglas,*
>
> *As your birthday draws near, I think back farther and farther. There's the time you helped get me bombed on my 18th birthday, and the hours you spent trying to teach me to drive your 3-speed Ford, then there's the nights mom and dad went out and you offered a reign of terror. I can still plainly see us picking cherries in an orchard by a lake, and I can remember grandma tucking us in bed in the big old house after we played in the hay loft all day long. My heads going places it hasn't been for many years thinking of the times I spent with you growing up. You know its nice to have an older brother, someone to look up to, someone to imitate, someone to follow. So much I learned from you, without you really teaching. So I'd like to thank you for all that you've been and all that you'll always be to me, a wonderful brother! I'd like to give you a fabulous gift for your birthday, but as so often is the case, money isn't there. So I'd like to give you something else, or I've tried-a memory possibly, I'd like to have you know, I loved growing up with you, and I love reliving many old times. Happy Birthday, Brother Douglas, Always, Brother David*

Yes, Uncle David is prone to being super sweet, and he's likely the nicest person you'd ever want to meet. His affection that he offers so willingly above is genuine; because that is the kind of person he was and is. That same gift for writing that my father and I share—creating art of most kinds, I'd guess—is present in him in spades. But the darkness that was in my father, myself, and some of my uncle's other siblings seems to be absent. In any case, I'm glad he didn't imitate my father much at all after their period of growing up together, and went on to live a good life. My father was not a good husband, or a good father, but he seems to have been an excellent brother and friend.

CHAPTER 3: THE CATS IN THE CRADLE

For 1972, there was an entire yellow pad that was 95% blank, and 4% ramblings or curse words scrawled across pages. But there is one extremely creepy short story dated 1-3-72 that's written as if it's an actual recounting, and not a dream. If so, then Dad is seeing ghosts.

I had watched television most of the night. They had been exciting shows, unreal….macabre.

I had just gotten to bed. A neighbor called her dog, a train whistle sounded, not too far away. My wife, Christopher, was close to deep sleep, having failed in her attempt—however mild—to get me to cuddle.

I heard a knock at the window – we are on the second floor. I didn't believe it. I heard the knock again.

I hesitated, then got slowly out of bed. Halfway to the window, I hesitated again, listening., but heard nothing, as I peered from the window, trying to separate the darkness.

I began to see the distinct outline of an arm
Disembodied
Just below the elbow, and still bleeding.

Crazily, there is nothing at all about this story, or near it that explains if he thinks this is real, or if he was dreaming, or if it was all fake and he wrote it to scare friends with the next time he tossed back a few beers. But the disquiet of the words, even the way he writes reminds me of my own scary tales. I have to admit a good potion of my writing talent must come from my father.

The next diaries date from January 1973 to June 1974, written on a series of engagement calendars (when that term still meant appointments. Some of the writing is my mother's, and some my father's. I can only conclude that this is one of the only calendars they shared in their lives.

January is mostly blank, the only things of note that my father is in court again for some issue. February is full, but more listings of parties, especially at new bars called Michael's. Honky Tonk, and Inferno. Valentine's day is "an emotional day for me,

Poem and Prophylactics." He also quit his job on the first of the month, and went on unemployment. He seems to have thought this was a good time to buy a camera and another car, as he bought one the next day, a Plymouth Cricket.

March is Grateful Dead in concert in at least three different cities across New York State, mescaline, acid, some woman named Diane he's sleeping with, who he's stayed with some nights and has a kitten. Two days later the kitten is dead, no reason given. Most of the writing is hard to decipher, some in swirls and doodles.

The month of April is even more crowded with notes. Thankfully many of the entries are printed and clear, no longer slanted after the 6th, the day my father puts serious money into his Jaguar: "fix distributor and carburetor, also oil and heater fan, hood catch adjustment, muffler patch and clamp." Yet 2 days later the "jag still runs shitty." Yet it runs well enough to do "71mph in a 55mph" zone the next day where Dad gets a ticket, "fuck." He puts a lot more money into his car and camera this month, which doesn't seem to do much for either. He tries to "start jogging and quit smoking again," but "gains back the 2lbs" he lost by month's end. He's working nights, but where is not listed, but still goes out most nights to party, sometimes waking up on people's kitchen floors. He's also sick for days at a time, something that began back in January, likely resulting from so little sleep and so many drugs.

May is busy, Dad's doing public service as a result of his offenses, and not happy about it. But he is somewhat healthier, "exercising every day." He's also getting stoned at work, and still putting money into his two cars, neither of which still work well.

In June, speed gets added to my father's list of drugs he's taking regularly. He and mom are also looking at houses, as their landlord raised the rent on them several times.

July is the beginning of a new job at a "new plant-lots of new rules." I think this is at Universal, a local factory. Dad already hates the job by the next day though, and is back to partying the following week. There are several days he writes he "was up to late to do anything" that day. Around this time he buys a motorcycle, which also doesn't work, which he tries to fix in between more parties and women. Mom, meanwhile, is working, keeping house, and trying to do everything right, including elaborately embroider some of dad's pants.

August is more "up too late to do anything," but at least the motorcycle is working enough to go for rides, dad's working some, and mom is starting to get fed up, walking home from some parties because he refuses to leave. Dad also begins using hashish and takes up fishing, something he's never mentioned until this month. He's also in line to buy yet another sporty car that doesn't run well, a Ford Falcon.

September is also busy, but there's a new sadness to the writings. Dad is trying art, specifically painting and drawing, and spends 30$ for art supplies on the 28th, a lot of money then. Some law went into effect, which makes Dad "box up all drugs." It must not have done anything meaningful though, as he's back doing acid, speed, and hash later in the month. He's also making a lot of T-shirts for people, I think drawing on them with markers that are permanent, as I had some of these when I was very young that my mother made me. On the 29th, an odd entry: "My heritage, a 100-yr old piece of cloth, a 12' goldfish, and a 400lb frog, instamatic apart and amazingly together." I'm going to take a leap of faith and assume he's writing while stoned or high.

October gives me pause, on what would be the last day of September, my father has printed in oddly apprehensive font, "THINGS ARE CHANGING. Something is going to happen, I can feel it and it knots my stomach." I can't help wondering to myself with a smile if he can tell mom is about to go off her birth control pills. There's no notes about this except on the 26th, it's a "Bonus Day-C paid!!" and also in a different color and sized a big bigger, "C not pregnant."

November is more parties and drinking, but some consequences finally happen: a friend totals his car while driving impaired, and Dad has been late so much to work and missed meetings without calling that he is let go: "Goodbye Job." Someone also hits his Cricket. He goes back to work with his father at Overhead Door.

December has nothing noteworthy, but in January of 1974, he writes in large red letters, "I'm going to be a father!" February he is working on buying a house with mom, and on the 19th, they close. He's also been buying and selling stocks these last few months, like Robintech. There are writings in the following months of working on the house, but not to pretty it up: Dad is ripping out walls and the attic floor, then doesn't have time to replace them with new wood. These remained the same for the rest of his life.

As my mother's due date nears, there are more baby writings, notations of Lamaze classes at a local hospital, and baby names. I would have been Joshua, if I'd been a male. Dad was pushing hard for Jacob as an option, as well. Then I am born, my name in large print on my birthday. The rest of the month there is notations of me crying, my first bath, and mom being pissed amidst more parties, bars, drugs, and drinking. But in the next months, Dad seems to be trying. He insulates and fixes my room and two others. But he also takes out the bathroom sink and walls, something that also remained that way until he died. My father also got a dog, there's notations of dog pen, and that "dog learns slow." He admits "I've changed some, I realize." He names the dog "Nameless."

In October, my father notes, "I'm 30, I came in working, hard times are just the other side of good times, and don't you wish good times would come, and don't it seem a long time...the scales should balance. Start to realize the seriousness of problems between girls." Because mom is pissed, Dad is "not staying home enough," and what she put up with when it was only herself she won't put up with caring for a baby. She moves in with her friend Karen on the 27th of November. "C still pissed. I'm ready finally to start again on our beautiful, once beautiful relationship. Wait please wait." Then "C at least talking to me, maybe we can get together, I really could find no better person to share life with." There is another dog that he finds and brings home, that a friend of his names, "Hopeless."

December is the most repellent of all the diaries, because he admits in the entries that he has beat the two dogs, because they pooped in the basement, likely because he wasn't home to let them out. "Nameless <develops> a bum leg, too long in one spot? Beating?" This also likely means he tied them up. A week later is the first new mention of them: "Dutch helps me feed dogs, first time in 5 days." There is no further mention; not that he gave them away, or let them go, or killed them, or anything, which makes me fear whatever happened was too awful for him to record. Dad, I can forgive you a lot of things. I don't forgive you for this atrocity. When I die someday my spirit is going to come find you wherever your spirit is, and give you a beating, if it's in my power to do so. And after that….I still won't forgive you this.

This year ends with the last notation in large letters, "Well, Go Then!" Mom had come and asked for the charge cards, and her personal property (most of which he wouldn't give her) and she and I moved in with her parents. Four days into the New Year, my mother asks for an official separation.

***

I always thought my father took drugs to have a good time, to loosen up, the same reason a lot of type A people get into drugs or alcohol. But while I believe he got into drinking for those reasons, his drug use was for a far more pragmatic reason: he didn't want the good times to stop because he was exhausted. And this need, which began in his youth and remained central to his life, was one of the key things that doomed him.

Mom seems to have found in me a reason to stand her ground; among the diaries of my father's I find an identical calendar to his that is mostly empty, begun just a few months before my birth which contains only her writing. Unlike my father's, the only things listed on it are appointments. She took almost nothing with her when she left my father, this calendar seems to be one of the things left behind. Later she asked for pictures, clothes, etc., which he refused to give her. I found all of these things she wanted then in his attic in boxes after he passed, all of it filthy, chewed into squirrel or mouse nests.

***

1975 is missing. Dad begins writing again in 1976, on both a calendar and on his soon-to-be favorite, yellow legal pads. Oddly, the legal pad is used only in November of that year, when he writes what seems to be a poem a night for several weeks.

January begins "with a work day, very productive-made tomorrow possible." He receives his "biggest ever paycheck, 1001.00\$." The month is a cold one, where it's well below zero some days. This is exacerbated by dad turning off his heat in his house, "food freezes in cupboards, only warm place is refrigerator, too much beer-couldn't fit, hang by heat vent." He says in several places, "if I don't get a woman, I'm going to go crazy," and "am I ever going to get laid?" Yet he's got Rosette calling him, and he seems not to want to talk to her, "call Rose, left phone off hook." He is taking welding classes at BOCES, a vocational center, and borrows twenty-one-hundred dollars, presumably to make good on child support for me and his part of medical bills per the lawyer earlier in the month. He's also been playing cards all month, after "making deal with God, ½ of everything I win goes to charity." After losing sixty dollars the night he makes this deal "pissed at God," he then goes onto win the rest of the month "God ok. and deep!" His winnings total a little under four hundred dollars, but he does indeed give half to charity.

February seems non-noteworthy; he is sleeping with a girl named Annie, welding, and partying. There is an odd poem at the bottom:

Whoever
Even the vans are patriotic
I grew my hair for the occasion
April is in the air
A bounce to the heart
The question remains, a question
Christopher, the enigma
are their others?
There are many…
There are none…

Listed nearby are my mother's name, and two other women, then a list of a bunch of names which must be friends/relatives on his mind, as I am included, last.

March is more partying, particularly at the Boston bicentennial 3-13 to 3-14, where dad "drunk and stoned all weekend, lose all my money, very few straight breaths." He is sleeping with some girl named Lynn for the first two weeks, who rapidly seems to have lost her thrill for him. There is a note, "<C> would have moved back if the house was fixed, what the fuck does she expect? A miracle?" He gets into "screaming arguments with mom and dad over Chris/Tara," but that does nothing to change his behavior.

April is empty, except for one note on 4-24: "Pick up my room, holyfuck, I can walk through it!", and a poem near the bottom:

> When I start piling or rather compiling
> The lost days I've wasted,
> The ½ days I've slept through,
> I astound myself with my laziness."

May makes up for April, as its full, the page written on all over in multicolor pen. He seems to have written most of it while high, but then most of the month he's partying. He also finds the joy of hot air ballooning, which in time will transform his life. He does finally "discover alcoholism 5-17-76," but doesn't again do anything to change his behavior after that stunning discovery.

...or maybe it does. June's header has the note, "Can't seem to stay out of bars, and its getting worse. It's starting to break my days as well as my nights...it's got to end soon. I never get anything done." My father, also a huge fan of Tolkien, also notes," The orcs still live. They become the debts, old ones, the bummers of life...the everyday people who can't accept change or other's ideas. <Chris's father> is part orc, and sometimes so is Christopher...and Tara is captured." This is so far from the truth its laughable, but this is the story my father told himself and me in my youth, that he was the hero, and those telling him to be responsible were bad.

July has nothing notable except an STD, which apparently got cured in a few days. August is also mostly empty.

September is "poor pay" for weeks, and several notations, "Can't see Tara, too tired/beat/too late/Mel tired, C too late." Also the notation, "an author or an artist would be nice." Sadly, my father had the talent for the former, if he'd have invested the time, he'd have made a good one, especially for his inherent sense of humor. Near the bottom is written:

> Do I have cancer of the nose?
> Do I <have beginning> cirrhosis?
> Am I mentally ill?
>
> A) none of the above
> B) All of the above
> C) pick any two

For his 32nd birthday in October, Dad buys himself a 1976 Toyota truck, ready to go. Toyota's were his go-to brand for worktrucks, and he had one until the day he died, even when he could no longer drive. He also finally sells the last of the penny stocks he dabbled in, apparently at a big loss, as there's a lot of swearing after that entry.

November is a crazy writing spree with 99% of the space filled, and I see now the reason why: dad has been following mom, "spying," and has concluded she "has a man, his name is a question." This conclusion and his resulting panic mixed with rabid jealousy has almost sent him off the deep end. The page is filled with musings about this other man, who he might be, dad driving past in other cars at odd times trying to look in the windows, calling from pay phones, suddenly suspicious when mom asks him to call before stopping in. The entries run from self-pity:

I rolled down the window to yell at her
I could see her roll down hers
but she wouldn't stop…she looked puzzled.
And as I started to yell the words died in my throat.
I spent the rest of the day <illegible>
I still love her so much
I am only just able to bear it.

to anger:

Where are you-why are you out with Tara, why didn't Mel babysit for you?
Tara is sick-why take her to your aunt's?
Your car is there, but are you?
Or are you just getting smarter?

There is also the poetry from the legal pad for this month, which begins with an apt poem:
What makes a fool? What is a fool?
A fool looks for greener pastures when there is already too much to eat
A fool gambles everything for nothing…

And a fool waits for dreams that come true only in dreams
And I find myself a fool tonight.

And another, which "is not prose or poetry, only my thoughts. I put them down to keep from going crazy. I can speak to no one." Dad goes on for pages and pages, working himself up to a frenzy.
Tara is learning about love from a stranger.
<Chris's> shades are open-to see out?
Has a neighbor? Or a friendly teacher?
Told her how many times I drive by her house?
She is looking for me…
She must know now the sound of my truck
And it warns her of my coming.
****
I know I've lied, cheated, done what she is doing now.
I was afraid to tell her the truth, that I might lose her trust, our relationship, her respect.
She is afraid for her life
She has to be careful
No wonder she humors me.

This is obviously insane, in that my mother didn't have any boyfriend at this time, she was busy trying to take care of me, deal with a new house that was another wreck, her sister's terminal illness, and raising a child alone who has repeated respiratory sickness as mom had smoked while pregnant. I also understand being sad or wrecked completely when someone you love leaves you…and you do usually want to kill them. But you don't stalk them. In my opinion, it's simply too much effort. But my father, who could not bring himself to stay out of bars, quit women, or stop drinking/smoking/drugs, begins to put enormous effort into his quest for knowledge, as if knowing will somehow solve all of this.

December closes out the year, all of the writings to do with either spying on my mother or being drunk, save a note on 12-8 that Rosette "just wants to be friends and Chris tells me there is no hope – this is my saddest day of the year." Oddly, there is note written by Rose where she actually says she wants to be more, that she knows my father is still "mixed up by Chris," and a bunch of other ramblings. Yet my far in the future stepmother has one other meaningful observation; "I wish you would speak more of your heart and feelings toward me. I read them in your writing, but conversation means much more."

***

My father had a lot of letters in with his papers that he had written to people and never sent. While some of them should never have seen the light of day - the one to me calling me a spoiled little bitch comes to mind - others were beautiful and heartfelt and should have been sent, not kept hidden to never be read. I think he must have felt embarrassed, or worried what people might think. Strong feelings of any kind, not just romantic, are admired in stories, and what we long for in our everyday lives. Yet we're deathly afraid to put ourselves out there, to show we do really care about someone or something important to us, to allow the power in the relationship to shift into someone else's hands.. This fear of vulnerability seems like a strange paradox even as it makes complete rational sense. Yes, if you care about something you're afraid to lose it. But that's all the more reason to say you care. Everyone will lose what they care about eventually via death: a beloved family member, a parent, a spouse, a child, a place, or a cause. Most people like my father will go into that eternal quiet without having shared their passions with anyone.

That is not going to be me. It's okay if my passions are not returned or even laughed at. They are mine, and what makes me feel most alive. Moments are fleeting, and once past, seldom repeat themselves. As my stepmother said, paper is a poor substitute for a living being, especially one who might be affected by your passions or share them. Make your heart heard, while it still beats.

CHAPTER 4: UNREQUITED LOVE

1977 is the first diary bound in a book that was made for that purpose, and reads more like a book, instead of a month with the highlights easily seen at a glance. It is only at the end that I see the inscription that Rose bought this journal for my father as part of his Christmas present in 1976.

My father was a hippie, if that's not obvious already from his actions and inclinations in the previous chapters. He states this year, "if there was anywhere in the world that I could be/want to be, it's anywhere listening to the Grateful Dead." In my first years, his hair was very long, below his shoulders. He finally cuts this on 1-16-77, as my mother tells him its either that or she won't let him see me: "I would never let it be said that I would let the length of my hair come between my seeing or not seeing my daughter." I believe this is the same 12" lock of hair I found when cleaning out his house, neatly wrapped in plastic in a paper bag, still clean. I donated it to Children With Hair Loss, where it was put to good use.

An entry 1-20 sums up my father's philosophy beginning this year: "Chris is on my mind most of the day, like any other day-I come home to an empty house and eat an onion. My bankcard is enormous. I am bored – I will go out." He is still seeing Rose and sleeping with her, but doesn't want to be exclusive or have any kind of real relationship other than sex. For Valentine's Day this year, Rose takes him to dinner and gives him a card and a rose, which he says is lovely. But this is mentioned only casually, with no real emotion attached. I'm guessing he spent the early evening being depressed, and the latter part out with her. Instead there is an odd Valentine's Day note amidst several pages dedicated to mom and broken hearts poetry: a page dedicated just to me.

Tara Fox Hall
In this diary of tears this page I dedicate to you…
May you never know in reality the sickness of mind
that comes from loving one who doesn't love you.
Your mother has known it, and I experience it now…
With luck you may never, never know the feeling of unrequited love.
But if you should, if that is your destiny…
There are some things that help.

Country-Western music for the time you spend alone,
Hard liquor for going out, and lots of work to fill the countless,
endless days...
Cigarettes and marijuana to smoke
And pencil and paper to talk to...

       I would call my father sweet and naïve to think that I'd never know heartbreak in my life, but most every parent likely wants that for their child. Work...I have lots of that to keep me busy. Other than that, I can't agree, as I hate country western music, I never smoked (bad lungs, remember), and people are much better to talk to when you're upset than yourself. But I would add the ability to see past your pain to a future where you're okay again, something that only comes from making it through your first broken heart successfully...one more thing he never told me, another that I had to discover myself.

       There's another dedication on the 17th, asking "whoever reads this, if I die, please finish my house as beautifully as you can. If you do I'll rest a little easier. If you don't...its hard to threaten from the grave." I can say although I didn't finish the house, I did what I could to donate and salvage what I could...and that the person who bought it from the state for the cost of back taxes appears, from what I heard, to be fixing it up, starting with gutting it and then finishing the walls.

       In mid-March, my father's "closest woman friend" Barbie dies. He has spent time on and off with her for years at parties and holidays, as I've seen her name often in his diaries from the beginning. She had an operation in the beginning part of the year in New York City, but it seems to not have worked. He spends time with her in the hospital before she dies, where she is in terrible pain, yet they are able to say a very moving goodbye before she passes that night. Afterward he and her other friends have a party that goes on for over a day and a night, only ending when they pass out from drinking and exhaustion. There is a strange similarity to my father's death, that he had an operation that didn't work, and died about a month afterwards in a hospital setting. Its also comforting to me that the "funeral" that we gave him—a party at his favorite bar open to all comers that went on for over twenty-four hours—would have been exactly the kind of send off he would most have liked.

Also in the diaries are little things that spark my own memory: the mouse puppet and other toys I loved as a child, my descriptions of my grandmothers in that one had a cuckoo clock, the other a lake cottage, and the ring my mother gave me with my birthstone which also happened to be my mom's sister's birthstone.

March 30th, my father's entry is a directive for me, for my life: "I want her to be prepared as possible for the life she will find here. I want her to be afraid of nothing -respect everything - love beauty in every form, not matter where she finds it. And love life - I want her to have patience and be tolerant, reverent and happy. And I want to be with her as much as possible. I want to cure her of her fear of loud noises and give her nerves of steel." My nerves are very good, and I have the other virtues he speaks of, though maybe not to the perfect degree he aspired me to become. But he alas didn't give me these attributes, because he was too busy with his own life.

April has Dad still sleeping with Rose, and his divorce from my mother is almost final. He's still jealous and angry, but back to partying. But interspersed in these entries of parties and drugs are finally entries of Dad wanting to be a father, taking me to see rabbits or horses, and have adventures, going to streams to look under rocks. He's begun going to Canada with Rose to her lake cottage, one of the places he was happiest. Unfortunately he's also gotten into drugs a little further, in that he's crossing the border with cocaine. He's also developed a taste for black beauties. His roommate Robby – who keeps leaving the burner on the stove lit – gets busted. Dad prepares to put up his house to try to get Robbie out on bail, lucky for him other friends raise the thousand dollars needed as his roommate is unreliable in the extreme, and Dad would likely have lost his house if they had not done this.

In May is my mother's birthday. My father gets her a book. He rereads it that day and does a joint instead of seeing her. There's a note dated 12-22-77: "I never gave her the book." Here begin again the hijinks noted in previous diaries, in that he locks Robbie out of the house, Rose tells this guy how to get in, so he does and gets all his stuff plus some of my father's stuff and leaves for good. "Rose wants me to write about her in this book…and wonders why I never do." And he's worried because my mother's going to the hospital for a case of strep throat, that she's secretly pregnant and going there to confirm it. Yet there's also a touching entry on the last day where my grandmother goes to his house, and spends the day with Dad on his yard, trying to clean up the nest of weeds and put in some flowers to make it look nicer: "With the help of Roland and Daryl, we get a lot accomplished."

In June, Rose moves in. "We have slept together for months and now it is a day to day thing with her here at my house when I come home form work, my meals prepared and often bought by her. It is a closeness that reminds me that she is young and playing house, something she has had little experience at. I wonder who will tire of it first and I know I will, even though I will miss the coming home to someone who cares. I may be throwing away another chance at a happy life. But would I really be all that happy? And it you have to ask, why ask at all?" Then in smaller letters, "She just came in." In spite of this rather cold entry, Rose and he plant a garden together using tips from my grandmother, which he works on periodically through that summer.

Over and over in the diaries, I have seen hints of my father's insecurity, from his inability to be a real partner for any long-term relationship to his coldness at any emotions other than his own. But finally there is a poem called Magic Shoes that says one more thing he never ever uttered to me; his sensitivity to being a short, wiry man in a world where tallness is prized.

It is a world of giants made for giants by giants
I look up to everyone and feel trapped
A large man's mind trapped in a tiny man's body
With no hope of ever escaping
The thought itself is paralyzing...the aloneness.
And women...what do I do for a woman?
Who wants to fuck a midget? Except another midget...
I tolerate their half-smiles and laughter to coexist,
but it is easy, so easy, to be bitter...
and to hate the world I live in...
And to hate my own body...
And everyone and everything in this fucking giant world.

In July, my father goes with my mother on their first date since she left him years ago. They see Star Wars and have strawberry daiquiris. He seems very happy, as well as entranced by the movie and the themes it represents.

In August my father cross-country hitchhikes to see his brother Terry marry my aunt Denny on a beach in California, leaving Rose and his mom to tend the house and garden in his absence. He leaves on the 8th, and there is no entry until the 31st, when Rose pens her first entry in the book she gifted him with: "…in your bed alone, still waiting for your glorious return. There are many things to be done around the house. The garden is harvesting, with no one here to eat it." There's also another guy, Roland I think, who writes an entry the same day who owes Dad money for a door installed previously, saying "I'm also loaded, I just talked to you and I'll see you tomorrow," so obviously Dad is on his way back.

Dad returns in September to find the house clean, and Rose completely moved in. From then on, there are a lot of blank pages, and not very many personal thoughts of my father's. I believe this is because Dad is aware that Rose is now reading his diary daily instead of sporadically, and doesn't want to share his emotions with her. I found a few harsh notes to that effect on random pages hinting at this. Rose pens a few more entries, asking my father to tell her he wants her. I believe she's looking to get engaged, something more than just be a live-in fuckbuddy who also cleans and cooks. There are frequent arguments, like canning of all their garden produce that needs to be done that he refuses to help her with that she finally does herself.

October brings a divorce subpoena from my mother, and a threat that she will cut off visitation until my father agrees. My father retains a lawyer to try to fight for custody. This was a very traumatic fight that lasted years, with my father trying to turn me against my mother by any possible means. I don't remember being in court, but I have my mother's diary she kept of my father's visitations, my reactions to him, various court appearances, and his lack of child support. Reading though it was both chilling and enlightening. Why did my father try for custody? He wanted to punish my mother by taking me; he had no desire to care for a child on a day-to-day basis and wasn't capable of the task in any way, shape, or form. I'm not sure what Rose wanted, if she thought my father having custody would make my father settle down and marry her, or if she was against the idea. My mother prevailed eventually, thank God. If she hadn't, I'd likely have been an alcoholic slut/drug addict who would already be dead.

By November Rose is still upset that my father won't commit, yet she still cooks him a turkey on Thanksgiving. When they are not having sex, they seem to be arguing. He is unhappy that while the meal she makes is delicious, she forgot to make him a pie. He further derides her in December for making a pretty glaring mistake about her genital anatomy. The next day she calls him a cunt for not wanting to have sex. Their few fights I witnessed while young were often laced with crude words and his cruelty to her; that seems to be the norm, not the exception that I believed the instance to be at the time.

December, my father begins trying to license a lithium lubricant under his own name, "Doug's Dynolube." I will testify this was fabulous lubricant that I still use to this day on a lot of mechanical things. A little lasts a long time, and he gave me some many years ago, but almost I ran out of it a few years before he died. Thankfully when I cleaned out his house, I found a half case of the stuff, which should last beyond my death. I find it funny and somehow comforting that someone may then inherit it from me and also think its great stuff. He's also looking into buying a space, a former place called "The Grange" in partnership with Rose. There are entries of getting art framed for it, and also plans for craft fairs there. I believe this place may be what he eventually called "Last Exit," a store out in the boonies that had hippie crafts, like string art, handmade Native American leather crafts, crystals, embroidered bags and shirts, carved wooden jewelry boxes, and fantasy/Sci-Fi items, such as magazines like Heavy Metal.

Christmas is "Beautiful." Dad is late buying presents "as usual" on the 24th, then "up to 4 in the morning wrapping" them. But he gets to my house at 10:30, where mom, me, and his side of the family have congregated. He speaks of presents he got, which finally gives a specific date to the three varnished wood plaques I have hanging on my living room wall. These were made from illustrations from a Tolkien calendar from 1976 by my uncle David, I found them while cleaning out my grandparents attic after my grandfather's death, and laid claim to them. Dad said he wanted the one of Galadriel, but I said I'd keep it until he had his house finished. I'm glad that I did, or it likely would have been ruined.

The last days of the year, my mother goes out with my father's friend Nick, and tells my father. My father loses it and stalks them from place to place, but can't find them. He finally waits by her house and sees them come home, where Nick doesn't leave until 3am. He confronts my mother, who tells him he's acting crazy and to stop following her. He confronts Nick the next day who says he was just watching TV with her, and that my father's overreacting. The last entry says my father passed out several times on her front porch from lack of sleep and being upset over this before he was able to make it to his truck and leave. I'd think this was dramatization of what happened, but his deep embarrassment comes off the page, so I think this really happened.

There are only a few entries from 1978, all of them on yellow legal paper , likely because Rose decided in 1977 that another gift of a journal was not a good idea. The entries jump around oddly, as I stated before, I have no idea if I missed diaries in the mess of Repair Hell, or my father just wasn't writing. But the themes are the same: anger, loneliness, wanting someone who is not there. Yet now my father's longing has shifted off my mother to Rose, who has finally discovered that the way to make him love her best is to make him think she's not into him. And its working, as seen in his poem, "She":

She sleeps lightly at my side
No one's widow, no one's bride,
Younger than I am by ten years,
Yet has a woman's dreams and a woman's fears,
And when she sobs, a woman's tears.
She's changed my life in two short years
She's fed the hunger in my soul
And filled the empty ness, the hole…
Left by another woman's leaving
Gave me love and eased my grieving
I'll never repay what she's given freely…

There is one page where he laments not seeing me often, but its more humor and resignation than real anguish. Because the harsh truth here is that Dad has given up on getting back together with mom, and the idea of being a live-in father. His gaze is on the future and a possible new life with Rose. They go to Canada this year for a week, a trip he describes as, "almost everything I could have hope for, and in some ways, more." He muses on his return that he "never sought out one woman, decided that <one woman> was the one…have I ever had the strength of character to decide, this is the one." But for now at least, it is too late, as Rose seems to have moved out, and into her own place. She's also moved onto other men, and seems to be popular. Like before with mom, Dad is often checking on her whereabouts, driving past at night repeatedly and listing cars who are parked there and if lights are on, asking her who she's with, or checking out her personal hygiene supplies when he visits to see if she's had men sleep over. He's still going on flights with a fellow balloonist, Dave, which he really enjoys, and sadly still getting into accidents with his truck, this year breaking off the mirror when he hits a telephone pole. He is 34 years old this year, which makes Rosette 24, in comparison.

The years 1979 to 1982 are missing completely. In these missing years, the store Last Exit that he had such high hopes for has failed and gone out of business, much of the unsold items he either gave away or stored, some to be found by me much later after his death (but alas, not those crystals). Dad also fought for custody of me and lost, thankfully. Something also happened between Dad and Rose in the missing years, as they broke up and she moved out of his house, and into her own place.

We next rejoin Dad in 1982, for the second and last diary in book form, this one in a black leather day planner, the first diary that I noticed on his floor. Dad also has starred entries on days he had sex, both on the calendar and the actual entry on the day of the interlude. This is perhaps the hardest diary to read, as it's got a month calendar plus daily entries, and the latter aren't necessarily in order, crowded together and running into one another, some starred in different colors. Later in the journal he began putting in entries that happened in January '83, as well.

But back to those meaningful stars; like the female symbols he'd used previously with mom, these designate sex. Months where there are multiple partners, he's sometimes used different color markers or put the initial of the woman's last name. For January, there's a Betsy, who wants a relationship; Stacy, who likes adventuresome sex; and Kathy, who is also hoping for a relationship.

Rosette reappears in February, though, and once she does, its apparent that like my mother, he's still obsessed with her. I wonder if this is because she lived with him at his house for a while like my mom did and tried to take care of him, or because she was so young when they met that he enjoyed being her first real relationship, or because she was so sexually rapacious. I conclude probably all of the above.

It's only at the end of this journal that I finally understand that where Rose is staying is an apartment on Way St. This was a place in the worst part of town, where I went several times over the years when he and Rose were together. There was an upstairs apartment and a downstairs one, which is the one Rose had.

Dad is 38 this year, now formally an experienced garage doorman who not only does work with Overhead Door but also for himself, with men he hires and supervises. Yet he is still doing the same old tired routine of several women at once, the diary begins with a reflection on what woman in his life he likes best. His conclusion is "I would respond the way anyone would, I'll love the one that loves me most and treats me like it." He seems to be on call for Rose, helping her with broken doors, dead car batteries, etc., while she often makes him meals at her place. He notes on the 11th that she stays over sans sex, and it's her "first time back here." But she's with a guy named Steve, as well as a lot of other men, if even half of what my father's "detective work" deduced is true. But Dad's no saint. There are also a lot more women now that he's both single and without a roommate; various women come and spend time with him, usually watching TV (for clarity, remember, in his house there was only one TV in his bedroom, and only one piece of furniture to sit on while watching it, his bed).

January brings fights with Betsy, and disaster, when my father elects after a dinner with Rose to go up to Davy's and get drunk/schedule dates with two other girls instead of going home. His pipes freeze as a result, and it takes the rest of that day to repair them. But he's gone again a few days later to spend the night at Betsy's place. For the next month, it's a rat race between being with either Betsy or Kathy, sleeping with them both, but also going on dates with them both, though apparently he told Kathy he loves her. From what he writes, I'm guessing that she initially thought he was something of an underappreciated Prince Charming, and that having sex and confessing love was a commitment. But by the end of February they are arguing and she's threatened to hitchhike home from parties he won't leave. She's worked with him on doors, but doesn't have the right clothes, so is miserable in the cold. Most of all, she's not just going along with his demands for sex. Dad switches to Betsy for the next week, but after a lovely shrimp scampi dinner that doesn't end in sex, but a long "terrible ride home" in "snowy, blowy, shitty" weather, Dad is "pissed, I won't call her again for a while." This leaves him in prime form for a newly unattached Rosette, who has a fight with Steve and welcomes him back to her bed the day before her 28th birthday. But she is back with Steve within the week, and Dad is back to balancing Betsy and Kathy, both of whom want more of his attention and want to know why he's not available/home more.

March brings a few near misses, when Kathy shows up and almost catches Rose at Dad's. Kathy though is starting to wise up, and tells Dad she "needs more, etc. etc.," so he doesn't see her - "I didn't want the hassle", and spends the night with Betsy instead. There's a notation that he "feels bad about Kathy" when he does this, but in the context I can't tell if he feels bad he's cheating on her, or bad that she doesn't appreciate him more. He's doing coke regularly with friends, as well as the three women he's seeing. Dad also catches his first squirrel in a Have-a-Heart trap in his attic, something that went on for the next two decades, until he stopped bothering to use the trap and the squirrels destroyed his attic and most everything in it. They would get in via the chimney, or under the eaves, I was never quite sure, and wherever they were coming in, he never sealed up the hole, or put his things stored up there into plastic tubs (plastic or metal garbage cans would have worked just as well). But he couldn't bother to go through this things to store them better, or throw them out any more than he could bother to finish the house, and so everything up there eventually came to ruin. He used to take the captured squirrels to a large park at least thirty miles away, drive to the middle of a bridge, then open the gate. The squirrel would launch itself out of the cage and hit the water a good thirty feet below, then swim for the far shore. Dad said he did it this way, when at 10 or so I remarked it was cruel, because otherwise the squirrel could possibly bite him. I'll add as a final note that he caught 10 squirrels in 1982 by the beginning of December.

April has another close call: this time Rose almost catches Dad with Kathy. Dad is also looking into wine-making, another new hobby. He has to cancel sometimes with one woman to be with another. I am mentioned along with Mom here and there, though most times the notation is he is too tired or sick to visit me, or to be "much fun" when he does. He finally meets my close childhood friends, sisters Nettie and Trina, on April 15th for the first time; he will spent the next four years taking me and often them on various adventures, sometimes horseback riding, sometimes to the Chenango River to try to catch crayfish, but other times to a nearby gravel pit where we climb the mountains of crushed stone and take a few pieces of sparkly granite home as shiny souvenirs.

September is marked with a small notation that "Chris is upset as Rose has still not moved out…it's not easy." So apparently Rose decided that she did want my father in her life after all…or else this means that at my father's house Rose has left some of her things. This might account for the many towels with roses in various colors that I found in the attic and took for rags or dog towels.

There is also a huge fight between my father and his parents over my mother. My grandmother accuses that my father stood Mom up for dinner after he said he was going to meet her, and asked her to marry him again. I'm not sure what my father said in his defense, but my grandmother was not appeased. "Then she said I could take all my stuff and don't come back for a long, long time! I don't like being thrown out of places and mom did this one time before already." By the way he says this, my father has likely been thrown out of a good many places; I admit to having thrown him out of my own house at least three separate times that I remember. This makes me feel good, to know this angered him. I only wish it would have caused him to change his behavior.

October, Dad goes to Canada again with Rose and some friends, then to the last of this year's Grateful Dead concerts. Yet my grandmother's words seem to have made a difference as he begins to spend more time with me in November, and be better to mom, to the point that mom considers taking him back and eventually getting married again. He puts in some work on his house, installing a new tub, which makes him feel good. But Rosette is not pleased at all by this change, and puts effort into getting his attention back, making him elaborate dinners and putting out again. Kathy calls him to go out, but he doesn't call her back.

December is "cold, icy," and Dad's big decision is who to go out with on New Years and Christmas, Rose or Mom. Mom wants to go, so he tells Rose he can't go with her. But this is only after Rose tells him that she's off to see her boyfriend that day for sex. There is also a note that he has to buy 82 presents, as he was always overly generous, to a fault.

Presents…my father was an ace in this department. He really enjoyed giving presents much more than getting them, and would often go to extreme expense and time to get someone a gift if he really felt something for them…or wanted to get their attention. He dressed as an elf one Christmas and brought flowers to my mother's school out of the blue (they were not dating or together at the time). He gave me 100$ one birthday when 10-20$ was the normal amount given by parents. But perhaps the most stunning gift was one that cost him something far more valuable: his time.

The gift was for my tenth birthday, I think: a horse farm playset that's about 4' x 4', made of a piece of particleboard cut in the shape of an octagon. There is greenish stubble which is supposed to be grass, and several mirrors cut in the shape of water inlaid into the board. There are holes in the board around the perimeter, and also bisecting it like a peace sign; these are for posts and rail fencing, also made of wood, with holes in each so they fit together and charring on the tips to make them look realistic. There is a small two-room barn with wooden sides, and a roof that also fits together via grooves in the wood onto an inlaid wood floor; a little electric light that runs on batteries was hooked up to turn on and off. He made all of this himself. I can't begin to guess at the hours it took, just to sand all the rails and posts and get them to fit together to make the fence and put all those holes in the particle board the right depth, width, and distance apart. I was wowed by this gift, played with it a lot, and broke a few of the rails by stepping on them or falling into them accidentally, as the playset was so big that it took up a fourth of our living room at the time. I still have this playset, but it's consigned to my basement under a tarp, the wooden posts, rails, and building pieces neatly stored in a plastic tub. One of my goals in the next few years is to take a picture, and then email a few charitable organizations to donate it to them in the hope that a collector might buy it and thus benefit them, along with the lovely hand made barn that my grandfather made and gifted me that same Christmas. Setting up the playset will be a daunting task of 2-3 hours, which is the reason I haven't yet gotten around to it.

One of my favorite presents from my father was one that cost him nothing but his time: a cable bracelet. I thought that the heavy-duty cable he used in his door work was pretty because of its silvery color. So he would cut me a small circle, then crimp the ends together with one of his stainless steel cable joiners, which to me was also pretty because it resembled a lump of silver. I wore the first one everywhere all the time, and he made me more until I got to be a teen, and outgrew them figuratively. I had forgotten all about them until I found several stashed away in his attic in a box. I saved them both, and was surprised that decades later, they still slipped onto my adult wrist easily.

***

At the close of December, the jig is also up with his *Ménage à quatre*: Kathy has given up and got herself a boyfriend, and Betsy apparently called the cops looking for him, and they called his house, where Rose was, reporting to her that his girlfriend was the one asking. So it's back to Rose and mom. Mom and I are both sick, this might have been the Christmas that my bronchitis became pneumonia and I almost died; mom developed walking pneumonia from being around me. Dad says "I don't know what to do with either one of them, they are both sick and I'm catching it, too. I would have liked to have slept with them tonight." Dad also pays for sex for the first time; he wants to sleep with Rose, she doesn't, but says she lost twenty-five dollars and she'll sleep with him if he will replace it. He agrees.

The rest of April is blank, as Dad stopped writing for weeks at a time. May is also blank. June is blank except for a scene that reads like a story, depicting a crazy erotic saga where Dad goes to see Rose and finds her missing. The scene begins in the slot for June 21st in the middle and goes on for the rest of June, but there's also another part of it on September first through the fifth and in August. Oddly enough, I'm guessing it really took place on July 4th-5th, as it begins with Dad visiting me straight from work where I gift him with a patriotic potholder I made, draw a picture of him holding one of my cats, and play him the tune "America" on a musical toy several times. He's very happy with all the attention – he walks the wrong way leaving and Mom has to call him back – but "Rose had begun to infiltrate my thoughts," so he leaves to call her. She doesn't answer. He then freaks out, going to her mother's house, then back to her apartment, where he apparently has a key or the door's unlocked, as he goes in. She's not home, so he "chills a beer and takes a shower," then talks to a neighbor who tells him she might have gone to a new bar. Dad, not to be stymied by not having fresh clothes of his own, "got out some of her clothes and tried to dress as masculine as possible. It wasn't super but I might be okay if no one looked close." He has a beer, but Rose doesn't show. He goes back to Rose's, takes off her clothes, and calls her sister, who lives next door, and finds out Rose borrowed her car and likely went to see her boyfriend for sex. Dad is livid, and "went to the door and bolted it form inside...there by God! I'd know when she got home – if she got home." He chain-smokes in his underwear and listens to the radio until she arrives at 1:30 in the morning. She uses her key to get in, but can't get past the deadbolt, so she knocks. There are several pages of dialogue, most of it raunchy, where Dad refuses to let her into her house unless she agrees to sleep with him. She is "amused and smiling" throughout this exchange as she admits to being stoned and possibly drunk as well.

Finally she agrees, and he lets her in and they have sex, but Dad "still needed more" so tells her he wants her again the following morning. She is sobering up by then and says no, but he won't give up bothering her because he "needs to get rid of this jealousy, this anger, this frustration, this hatred," and washes out the condom as he only has one in preparation. She is likely disgusted by what he's done as by what he's said—as am I—, and in the morning tells him to "move his things, so he won't have any reason to come back here. I don't want to see you." Dad is furious, and steals her address book, pulls out the phone plug, and leaves. He contemplates getting drunk, but goes back that night where she has him fix her washer, but otherwise won't let him near her. Mom meanwhile has apparently rethought her and Dad getting back together since the last journal because she lets him know she's interested in trying again. But all Dad can think about is Rose and "she does hurt me, more than she knows, with this Steve thing." Dad ends the long entry with the words, "why can't I learn? Chris loves me – and here I am alone again."

What to say, there is so much that comes to mind! First off, this entry confirms what I concluded already, that the sex Dad is constantly after has nothing to do with the person he's having it with; it's all about him, about how it makes him feel. His anger and the rest is all because he wants back the Rosette that existed back in 78': the naïve girl who would play house for him and love him no matter what he did, and was happy to stay home and wait for him whenever—or if—he came home, and be ready for sex anytime he wanted. People aren't "real" to him, they are things there to interact with when he wants to, and he doesn't know what the word love means, because you don't connive or force someone you love to have sex with you, or cheat on them constantly, or tell the lies to get what you want out of them. You can't ever make anyone be someone that you want them to be by force, or coercion.

There is also a poem I found hidden in a non-fiction book I believe I gave him about Antarctica much later in his life, as it's from a library sale, something I am prone to attending, but he was not. The title of the book is <u>Arctic Dreams</u>, which would likely be fitting for the poem. He wrote it at 8:16pm, 1-10-83, at Rose's place.

> My picture stares back at me from across the wall,
> Across time…to the future
> From one of those beautiful times in Canada.
> I lose myself in Canada.
> I lose track of time, as to how it relates to job, home,
> and the work I have yet to do on the house,
> The cares and frustrations of my everyday life…
> The push-pull, the hustle, the bustle…all gone…in
> Canada…with Rose…
> And now I look at myself – looking back at me, from
> a happier time and place…
> And I long to be back there…with Rose.

The other life lesson here is not to throw away happiness when it's staring you in the face, wasting time trying to fix something that can't be fixed. The past can't be unwritten, but tomorrow can be. You can't make someone love you, but you can love yourself enough to decide that you don't need to put up with behavior that's constantly making you miserable. Practice integrity, and treat others the way you'd want to be treated. And "by God"... don't lock people out of their own house when you don't even live there yourself!

CHAPTER 5: DESPERADO

The next set of journals takes place from August of 1983 to October; the medium is legal yellow pads. The beginning of this is more insanity, more a listing of detail from him stalking Rosette. Most entries are date, time, if she's home or not, if her lights are on, what cars are there, license plate numbers/makes/models of cars he suspects might be her lovers. He either has a key or breaks in sometimes, reading her diary, remarking on what's new (ex: "Marlboro's plain in all ashtrays including bedroom"; "she's back on the pill!"; "new multi-colored toothbrush over sink, Steve's number on sheet on kitchen table") and checking her douche bottle, remarking on if he thinks it was used recently. He also pieces together bits of paper from her trash to deduce that she's told one of the men she's seeing who is married that she won't see him anymore until he leaves his wife. This goes on until mid-September, when the entries finally change back to more of a diary form. He continues stalking Rose throughout this period, only controlling his urges to go through her things when he thinks he will caught in the act by her neighbors. That's only a momentary setback, though, as he just comes back under cover of darkness later at night if she's not home and indulges himself then. He also harasses her by demanding that she not take dates, such as her official boyfriend Sam, to social outings he's also been invited to.

Dad is now seeing a woman named Robin and another named Cheryl H. ("Almost afraid to get involved with Cheryl, she'll drive me nuts") for dates that range from Red Lobster to TV dinners complete with TV. He's also still seeing Kathy, as he brings her roses, a card, and Black Tower wine in late Sept., but she's still has a boyfriend. A new month brings different women: Candy and Gina. He's checking Rose's whereabouts is similar to his stalking of my mom, but this is more extreme. A few times she catches him: "Rose just getting out of her car, I waved, she waved and **smirked** – she couldn't help but laugh – I wonder what she was thinking? (I caught him driving by?)" Other times he wakes her up via call or in person to demand answers as to why she didn't call him/won't see him, or some other pretense.

He sees me in September to take me horseback riding; "I tried to go a little too fast-almost ripped my leg open on barbed wire

– just ripped my jeans-glad Tara didn't fall off." And he talks to my mother at the end of the month about disciplining me. October, he cancels plans when he is busy, and misses seeing me when he's hours late and Mom, I, and friends go to the park without him. He does see me finally in late October, "I would really love to see her blonde hair long. I've never seen it long and I want to! It might turn brown in a year or so and then I'd miss it forever! She's so pretty! I love her!" Yeah, as long as my hair stays blonde, I guess. He is late again in November by an hour, something I remember as the norm, so when he did see me, he often didn't stay long.

This was the first mention of my father's true love and passion of his life that he remained faithful to: hot air ballooning. This is the only lover he had in his life who he spent tens of thousands of dollars on that gave him his money's worth. In the missing years, he has studied with other pilots he knew, such as Dave B., and begun steps to get his pilot's license. He's also about to buy a small 1-passenger balloon and basket used for forty-five hundred dollars plus a five-hundred-and-fifty dollar fan from a mentor, Ron: this was purple, blue, and white with a striped pattern diagonal in diamond shapes. At this time he's just beginning his pilot training flights at hundred-and-fifty-dollars each, something he has to log before being issued a pilot's license so he can fly solo, the first record is an entry from 9/9, his "1st landing with help on ridge, then final landing by myself in horse pasture, we walked it out ¼ mile. Suburban Propane to see how tanks are filled." The next entry from September '83 is his 7th, by October 20th he's up to 10th. He gets a call from Dave telling him to go to IBM, a huge local computer business that is booming at this time, and he "drops everything and goes…it was worth it!" where he and Dave "take off in front of 1000 or more people, go up 750ft per minute." He flies again later that day, then goes back in the evening to witness another flight at a local park. Of all the years I have read thus far, this is the first time he has ever seemed truly happy or excited. Following entries show the same joy and wonder. He finally pays off the balloon 2-28-84, and takes possession of the fan and balloon. "It's mine!"

My father is not concerned at all if anyone else is happy, or what commitments he might be breaking in pursuit of his goals: he contemplates screwing his best friend's wife "She likes me – I can tell. But I could never fuck her because of Dave, I love him." When

Rose defends her boyfriend with "he's a good guy, he's good to me," my father's reply is, "He's nothing to me, don't you think I have any feelings?" It doesn't matter to him at all that he and Rose are not in a relationship anymore, or that he berated her for moving in with him in fall of '82. He only sees his own feelings; everything is one way. This would be normal in an adolescent teen or a child, but my father turns 39 this year. When my mother scolds him "friends, you worry about your friends, she said. Friends take better care of you than lovers!" is his response. He makes further comments about other good friends' wives "My secret desire is to make love to her, but I doubt I ever shall."

My father was also terribly self-conscious of his looks in addition to his height, something he doesn't make mention of until now. He reports that a young woman, Holly, "She said her girlfriend asked ' is he handsome?' 'No, not really. I wouldn't say he was handsome.' But she said it more nicely than anyone else I can remember – I like her! She's only 19!" She's also the daughter of his best friend. But if a woman does comment on his looks, even indirectly, my father is very offended: "He thinks I'm ugly, etc. – she lied and told him she never went to bed with me." He worries about STDs: "I don't have any desire to fuck her, I think she has herpes…She had a big cold sore in the corner of her mouth - I couldn't wait to get home and wash my mouth," yet has reported having cold sores, crabs, and other signs of diseases himself previously in his diary.

This is also the first time he has regularly written down dreams besides erotic recounting. There is something eerie about them, in that they resemble some of my nightmares in their elaborateness and detail, almost mini-stories. As the journal goes on these become absent, as he's likely started to keep them on a different pad separate from his journal. Later stories are fragments, mostly grotesque and crude ramblings written for various girls in some kind of effort to entertain them.

My father also installs a burglar alarm and gets a roommate, Tony, as he's had breaks ins with being gone from home so much. There's nothing else listed on stolen goods except that Tony and other people set off false alarms to the point the security system is angry with Dad.

There was erratic behavior in all his journals, but we see him really getting off the deep end here, likely because he's not gotten laid in at least a month. "Got an idea to bail out a whore from jail, she was picked up Sunday night, Karen, I'll call lawyer tomorrow – this could be a mistake??!!" Also, the gang bang I saw noted years ago was real, one of the men at it berates my father about it: "Danny gave me a hard time about that girl, the one I took out of the gang bang how many years ago?!" He flips out when he finds a Mom's new boyfriend, Mike, still at Mom's house when he brings me back, as if she belonged to him. "How sure of himself he must be to just be there at all. That kind of sureness is usually only bred by intimacy…This open statement of their feelings…was the final reality for me, the end of the last hope, I feel for her as I feel for Rose, just a cold hatred and the desire to hurt back and the patience to wait." Sadly, Dad will marry Rose soon after Mom marries Mike, both relationships will last no longer than 1-2 months before ending in divorce.

In November, my father suddenly becomes much more attuned to seeing me, because my mother begins seriously dating the man, Mike, who will one day be my stepfather. Suddenly there are now pages and pages of him worried if she's sleeping with Mike, is he staying over, and he's stalking her house again too, noting if there are cars there or lights on. He's surprised when Mike shows up before he's left to take me and friends for visitation for the day "Mike's got balls…and gall." Yet he's still trying to lay Cheryl "She's a pain in the ass with her constant <needs> - all take and no give. She doesn't give me anything unless she didn't want it in the first place." Sadly, this is the beginning of his liaisons with women like her who use him. There is a list of her asking for things, and Dad protesting somewhat but giving almost all of them to her, except some pie my mother made him.

He does finally visit his friend Barbie's grave, and is sentimental, says he can feel her presence. He also sleeps with one of his bosses' wives, his first sex in months, "two stars and a moon!"

I am also getting older here to the point I no longer am wowed by a father who appears with presents and wants all of my attention at a moment's notice but can't be bothered to show up on time or be there for anything that matters. When I tell my father on a visitation, "We'll do ½ what you want to do and ½ what I want to do," his thought is "I wasn't into compromise but I let it go for the time being." Why not, as his real purpose that day is to find out where my mother was spending her nights, "Tara didn't try to evade the questions entirely and she was as truthful as she thought she could be without getting her mom in trouble. I kept it light and really joking." Oh and also to get a little sex if possible from a new girl. He takes me ice-skating at the home of her mother, and I fell asleep while he was making time with Kathy, who has finally left her boyfriend for good. Later after he takes me home and questions mom some more about where she spent her previous night, afterwards he visits Rosette and makes out with her.

Rose is also being nicer to him, likely because his focus on her decreased after his new interest in Mom's business. She begins coming over and making him food, calling him again and going out on dates.

Lots of horseback riding notations, at six dollars a person for an hour trail ride, until this year, when rates jump to ten dollars per person, and my Dad takes me alone when we go from then on. But we still went to McDonalds for fries for me and Danish for him afterwards, a ritual I had forgotten all about until reading these journals.

***

The pad ends in mid-March of 1984, and there is only one further entry for that year, from April 19th. This is the one page I wanted to keep, as it embodies what I hoped to find reading these journals: some sign of my father's love for me.

> This has been a real good month for me, not money-wise but happy-wise. Yesterday a lady called on the phone to tell me they are ready after (4 years+) to go ahead with the low interest loan to do my house.
> But the real reason,
> the only reason
> I'm writing in this pad tonight
> Tara made me feel very proud
> So proud of her it made me cry.
> In a test she took at school which included an essay question,

she got 100%,
the only person in the whole school district to get
100%
and the test had to be graded by 2 teachers, to preclude
the possibility of favoritism
and right after she wrote that, she wrote me a note
"Dad no one can replace you, not even a king."
And that made me happy, really happy.
Thank you God for blessing me with Tara
And for the feelings she gave me tonight.
Thank you again, I'm doubly blessed.
We went to Chuck E Cheeses tonight, Trina, Tara and
Nettie, and stayed until 10:15. Tony had raised hell
with the girls earlier, and now they are out for Easter
vacation, and I wish my happiness and theirs could
last forever…

I laminated this page, and keep it separate from the other diaries I put away, even as I'm aware that the entry is based again solely on his feelings of pride and happiness. He doesn't thank God for making me smart, or mention my mother reading to me, or all the tools, blank books, and time she spent to help make me both an excellent student and a good writer as a child. But he does wish for my happiness, and that's something. It is also the only entry I can find in all his journals that is completely happy.

***

Years 1985-1989 are missing. In those years I became a rebellious and often depressed teen. Dad got his ballooning pilot's license, began attending a lot of balloon festivals, and eventually married Rosette 9-26-87 in a ceremony I attend as a bridesmaid. I found several albums in with his things, one of which was their wedding album. My mother divorced Michael after their brief marriage and moved with me to another house on the other side of town, near her parents, and swore off men for the next ten years. My father also divorced Rosette after a few months after she left him for another man she got pregnant by.

Dad also went to Antarctica for several months the fall and winter of 1988 to fix garage doors at McMurdo Station as part of Operation Deep Freeze, an update restoration project for Scott's Base. Dad wrote me a letter and sent a card that said, "Happy New Year," but had a note in his Antarctica workbook asking Rose about a Christmas party, so I am guessing that he was there for two months and returned by Christmas. I tracked these down, and include an edited version below:

11-8-88 (Down here they change the date to read the day first, 8*11*11)
Dearest Tara,
     I just finished my laundry, its 10:32 at night. That would be 5:32am your time (the day before). To figure out what time it is here, add one day and subtract 7 hours.
     The work day here is 7:30 in the morning till noon. Then lunch till 1:00 then work till 5:30. There are also 2 breaks, about 15 minutes each for coffee or hot chocolate or whatever (1 at 10:00, 1 at 3:00).
It's still pretty cold here. 0 to -10 + chill factor. It can be -50 when the wind blows, and it blows a lot. The weather changes quickly here – sunny with no wind to very windy in a half hour or less. I usually wear cotton long underwear then heavy pants liners then field pants with suspenders and belt: on top; a wool shirt with neck scarf or dickie and down parka. Oddly enough, I often only wear wool socks and sneakers.
It's kind of lonely for me here despite the fact that there are over 1000 people working here now. 1 of the friends I just got to know (my roommate) Bill G just left for the pole. I will miss him (but I already grabbed the extra blankets he left behind).
     I will try to get you some official paperwork tomorrow, something to give you an idea of how it is. There is a TV here, but tonight it wasn't working. Just as well, otherwise I might have put off writing! It's 11:00 now, and still bright daylight outside. You close the curtains tight to sleep. The food is good with 2 desserts every night but sometimes they aren't that great. Tonight's cake was sort of burnt on the bottom and the butterscotch pudding, although tasty, was the most unappetizing color.
***

11-10-88

It's 11:30 now and I'm just getting around to writing. It started off real cold this morning, but by tonight it was nice enough to walk around without my parka.

Water is still in short supply here, mostly because there's so many people (over 1000 last I heard) and all the water is distilled from sea water by huge heat treatment devices. I haven't seen them yet, but I understand they heat the water to steam, then cool the steam to make fresh (pure) water.

They figure it costs 50 cents a gallon to make and everyone (even with rationing) uses 7 gallons per day (Toilet, brushing teeth, washing hands). So that's over 7000 gallons if nobody wastes any. Besides you have to drink a lot of water here, too – they say 3 glasses a day – to keep from getting dehydrated in this "desert" environment. I miss baths and or showers.

***

11-14-88 (Sunday)

Not much going on today. I got up late at 11:30. It's great to sleep in! Then "brunch" – fresh watermelon, grapes, canned apricots, French toast, and apple juice – I don't eat this well at home!

Then I cleaned up my room some – then down to Scott's Hut – the original hut built by the Scott Expedition. Still in good shape – there are cans of biscuit mix on the shelves and everything was left as it was <back then>.

Then I climbed a hill and took some pictures of McMurdo and a statue. This afternoon, I organized some of the things I bought at the ship store, and tonight I watched a movie. It's 11:00 now and I'm going to bed. Tomorrow we'll be back working 9 hours, and its good not to get run down.

There are things here called fuel bladders and fuel pods. Fuel pods look like extra large bean bag chairs filled up completely round. Fuel bladders are like big yellow baggies twice the size of your garage as far as rectangular, but only 2ft high. They use these to store fuel in. They tell me that it takes 5 gallons of fuel to get 1 gallon of fuel to the south pole. That makes fuel pretty expensive. And fuel is what runs the generators to provide electricity and warmth. I can't imagine how much money they must spend here daily on just fuel, water, and food for over 1000 people…<I was told> $100,000 a week. But the importance of learning more about the ozone layer,

and the greenhouse effect, and the effects on the rest of the world by and from those things, I guess makes it worth any expense.
***

11-15-88
Hydrogen sulfides I am learning about today. Got to go to sleep.
***

11-17-88
Since I wrote <last>, my new roommate Brian H. form Woods Hole, MA has come and gone. He's off to the dry valleys to gather core samples. He was younger than I am, but already a doctor of oceanography. Quite interesting, especially talking of the plates in the ocean floor coming apart, the hydro-something vents, and all. But he was so advanced in his field that I could only comprehend some of what he talked about. Can you imagine creatures that have little gardens inside their bodies? They take in raw energy and chemicals, then use the energy to convert the chemicals into something that bacteria can eat and grow on. When the bacteria in their gardens are big enough, they eat them. That is a little about hydrogen sulfides.
I told him that was amazing. He said, "Yes, it is, and it doesn't get less amazing the more you know about it."
They call the scientists beakers here. I guess he would qualify, but he was a very nice person. Anyway, I'm alone again and maybe that's better than having one roommate-you get to meet many new friends this way. I will send this letter tomorrow along with a map of the camp. Love you, see you soon, Daddy

Late Nov '88
We come through here, reams of us, with our red coats and our orange bags, and we study this and we analyze that. The hope is that we can use the truths we find to change the way we live, to make ourselves and our children a better life. To be a part of that – even if it's only repairing the doors that go to the shop that keeps the vehicles going, that lets the scientists study and analyze this and that is to fulfill, somewhat, my destiny in life and give my life some purpose and meaning. For that I am happy. But it sure has been real cold.

That a man who didn't like to be alone without his friends, or to endure abstinence, or to limit his drinking or partying, or to be cold would knowingly put himself into a situation where he was experiencing all of the above because he wanted the world to be a better place than he left it says something very meaningful about my father, even in light of everything else he did.

The year of 1990 is also missing.

My grandmother passed away during that summer, and I'm very sorry to not have that journal, as I would have liked some stories/emotions from that time. My father loved her very much, yet my grandmother is missing from most of these writings. Perhaps, like I feel for my own mom, he simply couldn't imagine life without her and took her always being there for granted, because to contemplate a world without her was too terrible to make real by writing about the possibility. My grandfather, Dad's adoptive father, is still alive at this time, but he will pass very soon, in the next few years. My father, of his three brothers, was the only one who lived here all of his life or did garage work. And he was the only son to attempt to take care of his father and mother, as they slid into old age, ill health, and finally died.

The next diary is in the form of a calendar he must have got at Letchworth State Park, at one of his ballooning festivals. But its devoid of most detail, other then what drugs he used (his girlfriend of the time, Trina, preferred coke), how often he had sex, who it was with, and what $ she cost him, either in flat out requests in money for sex or presents/things he bought for her to get her to have sex with him. He's using her as a work partner at the same time, another way apparently to get back some of the money she's costing him, which just makes everything worse. It's also obvious that yet again he is sharing a woman with another man, and pissed off when she goes to spend the night with him. They argue and make up and argue again. Rosette is listed a few times, but the last listing indicates she wanted him to stay away from her and told him so. There's a scrap of paper with listings of cigarettes in her ashtray etc., so it may be that she finally had enough of his creeping into her house and going through her things when she wasn't home.

There is no notation of me at all, not even on my birthday, save a note "Tara threatened." This fits the right time frame for my first real boyfriend that I had in high school who stalked me to my school, and also around my house, sometimes leaving notes on my new boyfriend's car when he came to visit. I shudder to think that my father and someone I cared for had this creepy similarity.

There is only a tiny scrap of paper that I find from 4-30-1992, which reads, "I came up on them unawares with the new truck, her sitting and him standing by the 'lucky dog' stand. As I did he leaned over and kissed her nicely on the mouth, then they kissed again. Then she got up and went over behind him, put her head close and said, wait till I tell you…then she saw me. It was what I guess I finally needed. She never kissed me in public like that and not for a long time when we were alone." This from my memory is more feeling bad about Trina, when he took her to New Orleans and she elected to stay there with a hot dog vendor instead of return with my father. But she does return, of course, because he's too easy of a mark to pass up for a woman like her.

In 1993, Dad introduces Trina to a much older richer gentleman who joins their already crowded relationship, "Watching her fall in love again is very depressing for me. I couldn't face her today." She denies that there is anything going on, "He's gotta be 50 years old." But Dad himself is fifty years old that year, and starting to realize that he's missed on the most important parts of life. His house is still not finished, his two marriages have both failed, his daughter is attending college and no longer needs him, and his health is also starting to fail. He is still flying his balloon, in fact has bought a new one custom made for twenty-five thousand dollars called Blue Moon, and some summers has brought in more money with that than with garage door work. But he's never ahead enough to save any real money for retirement because he's always loaning it—i.e. giving it—to Trina.

1994-1995 are missing. 1996 is also missing, but there were two letters from lawyers dating from April that year which indicate that Dad was accused of criminal trespass, a misdemeanor, and hired a lawyer to defend him as not guilty. I'd guess his stalking his girlfriends by going in their houses and/or peering in their windows finally caught up with him.

His spending is also gaining ground, as his income, even with balloon rides to supplement it, isn't matching his expenditures. Ballooning is really a rich man's pastime, with all the equipment it requires. Hot air balloons log airtime like a car logs miles, and they are only good for so many flights before they need to be annulled again, in addition to any repair work from wear, burns, accidents, and customer damage. Like a car, there are bills for insurance, licensing, log books, etc. A trailer is needed to haul the balloon around in and there are bills for maintenance, insurance, and licensing on that. Arranging paying passengers is a challenge, especially in the winter months. Attending festivals requires a fee, and the submission of proper documents; while pilots can usually get a discount for taking promotional materials or agreeing to take a free passenger or two, his paperwork form the time always shows him declining this option. He's got six thousand in "debts and owes" in August, and even with paying some, two-thousand-twenty-five dollars remains. Where did the money go? He bought Trina an apartment and a lot of other things which he gripes about day after day, entry after entry, yet still somehow justifies that he's not being used "Someday its going to be better for me." He's beset by fleas from the cat she adopted then left him to take care of (which eventually bites him and gives him cat-scratch fever, which results in a hospital stay). He's terribly angry, and desperate, and yet still goes back for more. While this is poetic justice, as most of the things he berates her for like staying out all night, screwing 3 different people in one week, doing drugs and getting drunk, lying, and "using someone else's hard earned money" are exactly what he did to both my mother and to my stepmother, pretty much all the women he ever dated until he met Trina.

These are perhaps the saddest of the journals for me to read. I can't imagine being fifty, and knowing you've squandered your life. Dad might not admit that to himself, but an inkling is growing. He responds with anger, saying "Rose-Chris-Trina, you're all the same, always wanting more than I could give for your own selfish reasons – you'll never be happy – you take it out on the people you're with, and you're never really happy." But who is he really talking about? Himself. I can't speak for Trina, as she really was a drug addict and colossal flake (if a true animal lover and rescuer), but Rosette seems to have really loved him, and Mom did. He was the one always wanting them to jump through hoops for him to please him, for his own selfish reasons. Rose did finally realize her dream of being a mother, and mom found peace of mind with husband number three and me, her darling daughter. They knew there was a time when you have to give up, even on someone you love, and walk away.

The summer and spring of 1995, when I was in college, I went on two trips with my father, the first to New Orleans with just him and me, and the second to Florida, which included Trina, her son, him, and me.

In retrospect, both trips were failures that I should have known better that to commit to. But I had loved Anne Rice for years by then, and wanted to see New Orleans for myself…and I had no one who could either afford to go with me or had the free time. My father had already been down there multiple times, so when I asked him, he not only agreed, but set it up. The journey itself was memorable, and we went to all the important places, and stayed in the Bourbon Orleans, the best hotel in the French Quarter. I took along a video camera for this trip, and used up 4 cassettes worth of film. There were many good parts of the trip, but halfway through the trip we got into an argument as he said I didn't respect him— which was true, I didn't—and he really wanted to party, drink, and be out all night, and I wanted to be up during the day, not drink, and sleep at night. In retrospect I'm very glad I went, as there was probably no one better to see New Orleans with than him at the time, and I likely wouldn't have gone there again in my later life.

I had the cassettes turned into DVDs when the technology was available, and watched them after my father died. They began at the airport bar on our layover, where dad is smoking a cigarette and drinking a beer, and says funny things, like he's making a cigarette and alcohol commercial. My father was never polished, though he desperately tried to be. He's annoying sometimes in the many scenes that follow. But to my horror, so am I. I come off at times like a total bitch, even when we weren't fighting. It does not reflect on me as the best daughter or a nice person. That bothered me, just like the content of his diaries bothered me. During the year after his death, my feelings would keep me awake nights, my emotions like a prison of acid, eating away at me. And what do I do when something bothers me that I can't do anything about? Like my father, I write it down.

There is one bright spot, a letter dated to my mom that he never sent her that must be from early 1999, as its an ode to her father, who died in the final days of 1998.

"Christopher,
     I don't know exactly what to say. I'm saddened by your father's death. I didn't always like him. Sometimes I hated him. But I guess I always respected him. He always said what he thought and didn't pull any punches. He was a working man, like I am, and he knew the meaning of a hard day. He went thought a lot in his life, but he took care of his kids, and his wife, and his granddaughter, the best he knew how. He was a good man. All hard and callused on the outside, but a little soft deep inside for those he loved.
     If there is a Heaven, he's there.
     I got to make my peace with him a little before he died, when I did the work on his garage doors (Dad converted them from very old panels with a single cable lift to overhead doors with springs; he did the same at my grandparents' lake cottage). I'm grateful for that, and for his kind words at the time. He gave me a jack then, and I'll remember him by it. It's strong enough to lift a building. And that's how I remember him. I share your sorrow… May he rest in peace… Doug"

     My grandfather that he speaks of above was more my father than any other man, in that he instilled in me all the attributes that my father listed in his journal from 1977. I'm successful because of him, from all the time he spent training me, and teaching me to work hard, use my brain, never run out of money, and be smart about my actions and words. What did he give me that my father did not? His time. I have nothing he wrote on paper, almost no gifts he bought himself for me but a little Valentine's stuffed bear, and no videos of him except one brief clip. The morals he gave me to live by were imprinted in the countless hours he spent talking to me, telling me what was important in life and what was not by his action and example, teaching me what I needed to know to not just survive, but to flourish.

**

Dad was an optimist, as am I. But I'm sorry to say it didn't ever get better for him. His house was never finished, and got more cluttered and horrific as time went on. His cat died, and in time he adopted another stray one from my barn that my church's preacher had abandoned (yes, I left that church soon after this occurred), took care of it as best he could, until it died as well. I went onto college, then to my first job in 2000. I moved to the country, eventually got married, and have a great life I cherish. We didn't live near one another, and usually couldn't talk long before we argued, so we didn't see each other much.

His balloons failed their tear test sometime in the very late nineteen ninety's. I remember him calling to tell me, angrily saying that the test person had done it on purpose in the wrong way to make it fail. He stopped flying soon after, and the balloons sat in storage until his death. His trailer, which I am in process of refurbishing, protected them but itself weathered badly; I have hope to get it on the road in the next few years.

I found an odd letter dated 1-7-2004, written by my father addressed to himself at Mason with an obviously fake return address. Yet it has a postmark from being mailed, and the letter inside is addressed not to my father, but to one of the K sisters:

Kelly, if you are reading this, then it's already gone too far. I could see this coming a light year away. 1st you tell me you're gonna get money from your mom and you'll pay me back. Then its no money, we'll work it out.
<the letter goes on for almost 2 pages about payment for sex, how K is diseased, and using scam after scam to both avoid sex with my father and get money from him, including asking for money for an abortion because he got her pregnant. My father also indicates that they have had sex multiple times and ways and he's now infected from her.>
I don't see any pregnancy - I see another Kelly scheme to get money.
<He goes on to accuse her of several scams to get money from him>

I can't tell if ANY part of this letter is legitimate, or he sent himself this letter rather than accuse this paid lover of what he suspected…or if he thought she was somehow stealing/reading his mail so did this trick to surprise her. If so…what was he hoping to accomplish? It's completely bizarre, and I can't help wondering if this is when the tumor in his brain began growing.

I have letters found from a female inmate from March to May of 2006, of which the content is the expected pleas for help and sweet words coupled with graphic sexual scenes to elicit both sympathy and attention. She wants him to give her money, which he sent her, then graduates to asking him to put up his house for bail bonds. He refuses in the last letter, and she stopped writing after that.

In 2007, Dad is 64, and still trying for sex. His last coherent calendar is a page-a-day Escher, with notations of women he paid for sex, what they did to him, and what he paid them, if they also cleaned or cooked for him, what he watched on TV, outings, paying taxes, etc. He's still working and seems to be having the most sex of his life, because he's dictating the who and what by paying for it every time. There are at least 5 different women coming to service him, from sex to cooking to doing dishes to getting groceries to cleaning, and its pretty expensive at 25-150$, depending on what they do. But he only writes in it from January to March, the rest is blank. I do have one final note, where we went to see the movie Ghost Rider on 2-18 "Great Movie!" And on the last day of March, there's a notation about "1 more squirrel caught!" as well as declarations for love for both of the K sisters, who both have apparently declared their love for him, too.

The basement of his house flooded in 2011, and his furnace died. It was that following Christmas that Erik and I were uninvited for, approximately a week before the holiday. I called up my father to ask him where to meet for the holiday, if we could go to lunch the day after Christmas, as he usually spent both Christmas Eve and that morning with the K sisters and their family. His reply was that he had to install a shower for one of the K sisters that he was getting her for Christmas that day, and so couldn't see me until maybe the following weekend. It was at that point that I gave up. I remember him saying, "I told her I'd do this for her. Tell me what I should do? Tell me what you want me to do?" I remember thinking, *I'm done. If you don't already know what you should do, I am not going to ask you one more time to make time for me.* I said something like I'd call him later to make arrangements and got off the phone. Then I never called him again. He left a message sometime after, asking me to call to get together, and I never did. I took his presents and returned them all, and just avoided him. He left a bottle of scotch and a small box he'd made for me in the mailbox sometime that spring. I got a new locking mailbox with a slot after that that my stepfather helped me install.

I relented some years later, in 2014, and sent him one of the books I had written. He again left presents in my mailbox, some fox socks and a unicorn shirt. I also left cookies for him on his birthday at his house most years after that, but I have no idea now if he actually got them or someone else just took them.

Dad retired at 65 because of his health reasons, but because he'd spent all his savings to buy the two K sisters a house where he eventually lived in an upstairs bedroom, he had nothing to fall back on. He also had his constant desires for sex to satisfy which I doubt he gave up. He began defaulting on his credit cards, and going to various banks, opening accounts, and getting cash advances. When he began getting notices of termination or past due bills, or he was over his limit, he would abandon the account and move onto the next bank or get a new credit card. He stopped paying taxes on his two houses, and my grandparents' home, which they had left him. If he hadn't died at 71, he would likely have ended up homeless and broke, as I'm sure the K sisters would have kicked him out when they had fleeced him of everything.

I wish that I had the power to go back and write him a better end to his life, or better yet an epiphany, where he realizes he's been a cad and wasted his life in pursuit of things that don't really matter. It was probably always too late for him and mom; she became someone who would never have taken the shit he dealt her in her youth in her later years. But he could have made it work with Rose, if he had tried. She would have been a good wife, and probably a good stepmother, in time. But he wasn't willing to meet her halfway…or deal with the "role reversal" of a woman who was also a fan of open relationships, who wasn't afraid to have sex with whomever she wanted the same way he did. I wish he would have discovered the truths about himself to change the way he lived, to give himself a better life, one where he spent more of it genuinely happy.

CHAPTER 6: A REASON TO BELIEVE

Also included with no date were scraps of stories and also musings on a single piece of yellow legal paper.

"The way to make friends is to listen. Don't talk about yourself too much. Let people tell you about them. Sometimes you have to stop yourself from telling your stories, especially if it makes you seem superior because it will make others feel less important."

"Be interested in what others have to say even the ones you least agree with of respect. Often you can learn something important from the person you least expect to be able to teach you anything."

"Be polite, be courteous, be honest, even if others are not polite or honest with you. Learn to tell the difference without showing your emotions."

"Be especially nice to people who are nice to you and the people you really don't like. Avoid them but don't let them know you don't like them." I agree with all but this last, as I believe you should be nicest to those who treat you best. To hell with the ones that treat you like dirt.

There is also a poem that Dad wrote in December of '83 which gave me pause enough to list it separately here:

> I've got a lot of mixed feelings this holiday season
> And women of course are mostly the reason
> Maxine is the worst I think by her hand
> And she screwed up my good life at least one I planned
> Loretta's the best, the sweet woman of dreams
> But am I in hers? Is it what it seems?
> And Rose in the middle, at least as of late
> I just wasn't ready for that cruel stroke of fate.
> Chris the benign is gone and behind
> But feelings forgotten are feelings not mine
> Tara, oh Tara, you're my one lucky star
> The one girl I worship from near and from far
> If only I could find the one girl like you
> I might even yet start over anew
> Oh, perhaps time will tell which one is the one
> But I'm much too horny to have fun having fun.

At face value, Dad is listing out the women in his life. He's mad at Maxine for introducing Mom to Mike, Rose and Loretta he's bedding, and he's wishing that his girlfriends would be naïve as I am, happy to see him when he has time and inclination, with no real big demands. It's him trying to be funny. But there's a darker aspect, listing me at 9yrs old in with his lovers, with nothing to state he's my parent, not something else. This brings to mind the idea that my father only saw women as one thing, and he didn't know what to do with a daughter, the one woman in the world he couldn't have sex with. I'll add this lesson to the list of things he never told me: don't create poems that contain both your child's name and the word horny.

As listed previously, I am not a saint. I remember confiding a college affair with a married teacher to my father during lunch at some restaurant. He had admitted at the time that he was seeing a woman with a fiancé. We chuckled about our illicit relationships as a shared, warped form of bonding. The next time we fought, he threw my confession back in my face in front of my mother, who didn't know. That was the last time I trusted him with any information that meant anything to me, whether it was secret or not. This was also the first time that I ejected him from my home. I have always tried to keep my promises, any that I make, and strive to always tell the truth, even when it's hard to do and it would be much easier not to. This moral clarity makes a person think twice about their actions. I have made mistakes in my life that I'm not proud of, but I do own them.

***

There is also one final 2-page letter dating from 1991, on Easter Sunday of that year, which stays with me and is the reason I felt I had to write this book. It's a long letter to Trina, one he never sent. In with the following musings often repeated in his entries about coke and sharing her with her other lovers are the following lines:

> "I feel like a fool right now, because I
> believed you again, when you told me you weren't

staying over. Feeling like a fool doesn't mean much to me anymore. I've gotten used to it. The heaviness in the pit of my stomach, that still bothers me. The sadness I feel and the distrust."

"Whatever you do, don't change anything. Especially don't change yourself. You would have to be unhappy with your life to want to change it. You would have to be unhappy with yourself."
He lists her ability to get presents, sex, and money from multiple people and drugs and sleep in most mornings. "In a lot of ways it's a life to be envious of. Would I want to change that if I had it? Good question."

"I guess if anything changes it's got to be me. And as unhappy as I am with the way it is now, I'm afraid of being more unhappy without you. I love you so much that being without you scares me. I'm frightened with the thought of losing you from my life. I'm damned either way."

"I write notes and letters to you that you'll never see,
So you won't get angry,
And I won't go crazy,
And neither one of us will have to change a thing."

To me this sums up everything that was my father, and what doomed him: he refused to change out of fear, even when he knew he had no other way out. It's the greatest lesson of his life, and one I take to heart: don't be afraid to change. Pouring your heart out to paper isn't a substitute for taking action in your life to solve what is making you unhappy. Yes, there are always things you have to accept, but there's considerable freedom to change what things you can in your life. There is so much he might have done to have a more satisfying if not longer life. I might have had half-siblings beside his hospital bed with me, or maybe Rose. He might have quit smoking in time to escape COPD, to enjoy his retirement, however brief. Maybe he wouldn't have developed brain cancer in the first place, as my doctor tells me its not genetic. Maybe he might have been the father I thought he was when I was young, instead of one I lost faith in and all respect for. I can't say his life would have ended differently, but his life would have been very different.

CHAPTER 7: AFTERMATH

So what happened to the hot air balloons, especially Blue Moon? I found her nicely tucked away in the trailer he had bought to tow her to festivals. The trailer had been left outside, but was by some miracle still airtight, in spite of the layer of green mold all over it, two flat decrepit tires, and a huge tangle of briars that covered the entire thing. Both basket and balloon (technically called the envelope) were fine and unchewed, albeit a trifle musty from the almost two decades of being stored in the dark outside in wildly varied temperatures. The basket was missing a propane tank that had been left outside (likely to be refilled, and my father hadn't wanted to bother putting it back inside the trailer after he did this). Despite years outside in the elements, that tank also was fine, and I placed it back inside its leather holder, which accepted it easily in spite of not holding a tank in close to twenty years. Also in the trailer was a fan, and another basket for my father's smaller balloon. Inside the house, musty and mouse-smelling, we found two more balloon envelopes. One was my father's initial balloon he trained on before flying Blue Moon. The other I had no memory of at all.

My uncle worked on the trailer for several days, and got it mobile, then towed it to my house, along with a compressor with a leak and a broken power cord, and some special lights for working on new construction. This was necessary as we weren't sure after my father died what would happen, and if we'd have access to the houses at all. We needn't have worried, as they were not claimed for back taxes until the late fall. My uncle advised me to ask a few of my father's local friends for help in selling these. While that would have been the easy path, I wasn't about to do that. These were the same "good friends" who had screwed my father out of money in various deals for years (and that was from the little he'd told me of his many, many business dealings, so I am sure there were multiple others). I wanted to both repay my uncle and also get Blue Moon a new lease on life, not get swindled myself. Instead I contacted an owner of a local ballooning business via a mutual friend. I didn't know Sean at all, but he proved to be invaluable, both buying my father's fan for cash, and also hooking me up with an online ballooning forum where I was able to sell the balloons and baskets as a lot to an owner out west. He in turn sold Blue Moon to a lovely woman who loves her as much as my dad loved her. Seeing her fly again via pictures and YouTube was the best thing to come out of all of this. I couldn't save my father from himself. But I did save her, and get her out of that Repair Hell, and onto the life she had deserved. In some ways, that balloon was me, being given a chance to let go of everything that had happened and form a new life with people that would cherish me for what I was, not for what they wanted me to be. It was a big step in letting go of the past. I made my peace with what my father was a long time ago. But I didn't make my peace with everything he'd done until I wrote this book.

What happened to the houses? They were taken by the government for back taxes. I have yet to drive by them as of this writing, as they are miles away from everything I do now in my life.

And lastly, what happened to me and my uncle? You might have thought from all the help that he gave me that he and I became really close. Instead we had a falling out soon after my father died. The last time I saw him was already years ago, at my grandparents' home.

**

I had three uncles total, all younger than my father, and all from another father, from my grandmother's second marriage. I never knew my biological grandfather, only Dad's adopted father. My uncles and aunts never factored much into the diaries that I found, but the four brothers were always fairly tight with one another. I did find more than a few sweet letters my other uncle David had written over the years to my father. One of these was behind a picture of me. I'm five years old in the picture, standing in my grandmother's garden in a white fancy dress with a serious expression, huge dark circles around my eyes, and a face white as a sheet. I always liked the picture, even though I thought I resembled a sad little ghost in it, and it's one of the things I made sure to get out of that house. That little girl had suffered enough through the years (i.e., who knows what nasty business she witnessed from her dark little alcove in that almost lightless room?). But from the letter my uncle David writes, he says that day I was "excited and full of energy" and that the vegetables I am shown holding are ones I "Specially picked for my Daddy." My uncle goes on to say, "I remember the love she projected for you and in the moment of the actual picture, I <u>know</u> she was thinking fondly of her "daddy" and indeed was oblivious to her surroundings." In looking at that picture, I think it far more likely that I'm worried that what I'm doing to try to please my father won't work, or that I'm glad to be outside away from my father and mother, who couldn't be in each other's company for long without fighting and would always snipe at one another in the guise of joking. I also must have been either sick, or getting over a sickness, because of how pale and drawn I look. But my uncle didn't see that. In essence, this sums up the resounding difference between my uncles and my father: while he wallowed in the worst life has to offer and made his home there, these three spent their lives seeking out and enjoying the best life has to offer, with the best people, while doing their utmost to cover up all the ugliness that they possibly could. It has always amused me to think that were he not their brother, they not only wouldn't have talked to him, they wouldn't ever have crossed paths with him at all, unless they called him to fix their garage door.

All of my uncles had careers, and were married to women who had similar careers. They are retired now, and enjoying a luxurious retirement because unlike my father, they made good life decisions. All of them seem fairly happy in all they have achieved. I say that with distance because I don't really know them. Part of that is because they have lived out of state for most of my life, and part of it is because they never made much of an effort to get to know me. I have never understood families ignoring each other for most of the year that then send lavish gifts with many expressions of love and affection. Being in someone's life and being there for them in their not just good times but worst times is the strongest expression of love there is. My father always said that I didn't need anything from him and that he wished he could help me more. What he meant by that was more things he could procure for me. I did need a lot from him. Sadly, it was all stuff he either wasn't willing to give or didn't know how to give in the first place.

This family trait of being distant is strange to me, as my paternal grandmother was a wonderful person, always doing things for her neighbors, making me so many gifts as a child, and not being afraid of being blunt when bluntness was needed. She died when I was only in my mid-teens from complications with Alzheimer's, when I was on Disney vacation with my mother in Florida. My grandfather was almost always working or watching TV, but he was also kind. He died in my early twenties when I was in Florida with my father on vacation, again at Disney. I will add here as a footnote in this grim trinity that my father died less than a month before my mother and I took a trip to Florida to visit Disney World, our first trip back there together. I wonder if my dad would have died naturally while we were there if he hadn't taken his own life. I also am a little afraid to ever book another Disney trip to Florida.

I told my uncles after scattering my father where I had put him, in case they wanted to know his final resting place. I was actually funny about it, sending them each postcards I had found in his house branded Antarctica from my father, saying that he cared about them and was at peace and that he thanked them for all they had done for him. Only one uncle contacted me, clearly bewildered, asking if I had sent them. I replied I had, that I thought Dad was at peace, and wanted to convey that in a less than somber manner. Alas, another "joke" gone wrong. But with this one, I tell myself that Dad would have gotten the joke…and liked it immensely.

***

As I said, I had a falling out with my uncle. This happened because they penned his obituary, within it listing the woman who'd fleeced my father of his savings by name and calling her my father's "Special Friend." While I'd been able to deal with reallocating salvageable things from Repair Hell, sorting stacks of unpaid statements and calling his creditors to close accounts, and the grim hospital visits where he fought for breath like a bug-eyed fish, this was the straw that broke me. I lashed out at my uncle via email, he lashed back, and now Christmas cards and likes on Facebook are the extent of our relationship.

I saved his nasty emails to me, and mine to him, planning to put them here in my summation as some kind of vindication for us no longer talking. I even edited them and formatted them, going on a tirade again for what he said to me. But having penned this book, I deleted that entire section instead. There is no point being nasty to someone who doesn't care about you, or wasting time thinking about them at all. It's better to cut them our of your life permanently, and get on with your life.

Re-reading his emails with a few years of distance helps me to see that he was likely as fucked up by everything that happened as I was, especially his refusal to see the K sisters for what they were. That's no excuse for his treatment of me, which resembles most a manager trying to deal with a difficult subordinate employee that he doesn't care for. But he and my aunt never had children; that may have been the way he knew best to deal with people he wasn't close to.

In any case, he did indeed sell the truck, and I sold the balloons and gave the money to my aunt, who I met at a local grocery store parking lot, where she traded me for my father's ashes. My uncle sent me several other letters, trying to be cheery and friendly. I was short and to the point, and as intended, he soon left me alone.

I don't hate my uncle, and I have forgiven him for his nasty emails. I'm sure in his mind that he thinks that he didn't do anything wrong. I don't forgive him for basically abandoning his mother to my grandfather's care. How could he consign the woman who loved him and cared for him to beatings at the hands of his father? He was willing to step in to get power of attorney for my father, why hadn't he protected his mother? The Alzheimer's that took her life was very slow, and my grandfather took care of her for years at home by himself. I remember clearly the first Christmas after her initial diagnosis. My uncle and aunt got my grandfather a cocker spaniel puppy as a present, of all things to do. I'm fairly sure that my grandfather beat that dog as well as my grandmother, before my aunt found it another home. It's like they had no idea of how to behave upon receiving the diagnosis, so chose the worst possible course of action. Even that could be excused, but then to see what was happening for years, and to do nothing?

My other uncle and his family were out of state for all of my life, except for very brief visits on Christmas sometimes or phone calls on holidays. I cut off contact with them as soon as my father passed. I voiced this plan of mine to my father almost a decade ago, in one of our last hour-long phone conversations. I told him that I planned to cut off contact after he was dead. He said he understood my decision, and that he agreed I should. I'm not sure why I wanted his "permission," but it makes me feel better somehow, that I did tell him.

My father and I never talked of final arrangements, though I did mention it to him once or twice. I was reading a book called Stopping the Clock, about things to do to live longer. There was a quiz in back, which had you answer a list of questions, then told you how long you were expected to live. I got like 100 years, and my mom 90s. My father's answers calculated he should already be dead. He laughed it off, but it prompted me to ask him what he wanted. He mentioned cremation, then changed the subject. So all I had to go on were these diaries, and what I knew of him, which is why I spread him where I did.

I think my relatives were appalled I left him there, miles from where we all live. But from his journals, he spent most of the happiest parts of his life in the thick of the action, the life of the party. Someone like that doesn't belong in a graveyard full of somber gravestones and silence. He belongs somewhere people will be all year, where there's music, and conversation, where young lovers lose their virginity in the summers amid flowers, and even in the cold breath of winter, hikers walk the trails and feed the birds. He'll never be alone there. I hope someday when I die, someone will also take my ashes to that same place and scatter them, too.

I asked my uncle David once why our family wasn't closer, when I had such good memories of my grandmother. His reply was that he thought we were very close. It was then I understood how far away our definitions of close really were, and that this was as good as it was going to get. He sent us all an email last year, showing us in detail his storage system for his Christmas decorations complete with pictures, so thorough it resembled a work instruction. His brothers replied about storage options, and fairy lights. I went out to the local target, bought a light cord reel at ½ price, took a picture of that and sent it back, saying that I hadn't been aware that storage was so important a tradition in our family, but I certainly wanted to get in on the fun. The joke was not appreciated, and I'm reminded writing this that my sense of humor is sometimes very like my father's: probably not that funny, on the receiving end. I am thankful for buying the reel though, as it did make my Christmas prep a little easier. But I am resolved to think more about what I say and hold my tongue, so something I mean to be funny doesn't comes out sounding just mean, or cruel.

I'm not sure why these three brothers are so focused on presenting perfection, or why they need to impose flawlessness on everyone around them like a thick sweet sugar coating that covers up all the ugliness. I do know that I've had my fill of politics in the other areas of my life, I'm not doing them anymore in my family. Real life is ugly, and shocking and raw. I understand a learned skill to see the hope and beauty, to hold onto them and let the rest go, because focusing on just the ugliness leads to misery. Yes, there are conflicts in families and there's swearing and fights. But closeness comes from seeing all of people, not just the nice parts. Everyone has problems, some worse than others. You work on what's wrong together, not cover it up and look the other way. I wonder if my uncle or aunt had ever asked my father not to drink when he visited for Christmas, would we have been an intact family when my dad died? Or would my dad have just refused to visit until they relented, or brought his own beer? My extended family on my grandmother's side has a reunion each year, and it's mandatory that there is no drinking at it, no exceptions. My father attended with me one year, and everything was fine. I wish we had tried this at Christmas, at least.

Yes, there could have been extenuating circumstances for leaving my grandparents to end as they did. My grandfather was as stubborn as my father, and he would not put my grandmother in a nursing home. Even after she died, when he was smoking and drinking himself to death as a shut-in, he refused to leave his solitary existence. I remember my preacher uncle visiting, and his thinly veiled fury that my grandfather wouldn't take better care of himself, or listen to his requests to stop drinking or smoking. My father's answer to that was to hire a woman in to care for my grandfather who, of course, was trash and stole money from my grandfather instead.

In closing, the last lesson is this: don't give up, or put your head in the sand about a problem that you can't walk away from. It will just come back to bite you in the ass later. Spend time with those you love, while you still have them. Part of growing up is learning you don't know all the answers. But you only have to know a few to take action: who you are and what you really want, both for yourself and for the world. Then, you have to go after it.

EPILOGUE

I took a drive through memory lane today, going down to my father's old neighborhood where he used to live with my stepmother (a place my mother once said was the worst street in all of Binghamton to live). Way St. looked worse than I remembered, all of the shops that once were in the strip malls nearby had moved, leaving bare storefronts and cracked broken pavement. Others were dying, with only a Chinese food place left out of the thriving four stores that I remember. Others were completely empty. Businesses nearby were also gone, signs for lease and sale aged beyond hope that anyone would ever buy or rent them. In some of these were graffiti paintings by local artists, and some half-hearted landscaping, as if that would help the residents to somehow forget all the signs of slow death around them. I considered stopping at my father's old house at Mason but didn't go.

***

Thoughts of my father did lessen as time passed. I haven't forgotten the bad things he did, or the more fresh atrocities that I only learned about after his death. But life moves along and pushes out the past like a plow cutting a swath through a fresh drift of now, leaving a clean path ahead. That is maybe one extra last lesson, that remembering the past is vital, to not make the same mistakes. Be willing to forgive, but don't completely forget. Yet constantly thinking about those mistakes or concentrating on other evil that was done to you is just a shackle that keeps you from moving on. My father held tight to a lot of bad things that he couldn't let go of, and they ultimately destroyed him by keeping his mindset going in circles, making the same mistakes over and over.

There are times you can't help remembering, even years later, and it hits you like a sharp slap to the face. I bought my father two balloons when I went to see him the eve before his surgery: a "Get Well!" round one with flowers, and a pink porpoise, as that was all that was quick to grab that morning. The porpoise deflated very soon after, but the other lasted eerily until the night before his death. I popped it that day before leaving, angrily thinking he wasn't going to get well, everyone knew it, and the balloon was just a tragic reminder of his giving up. When I see balloons like it, I don't feel any effect. But the pink porpoise balloons still give me a chill. They are pretty balloons – Dad really liked his – but I'll never buy another one, not even one in a different color. Yet never is a really long time, a term we humans throw around a lot and rarely stick to, either in love or in hate. Time changes our memory and our perception of life events. I think that's a good thing.

I visited a Canadian friend before the pandemic hit, where we both attended a convention as writers to promote our work. Part of that journey, my first travelling alone, was to bring the Canadian coins "home" and take the last steps of letting go. I brought <u>Artic Dreams</u> with me, planning to spend one day that I wasn't promoting on reading it, and maybe even taking a trek outside Timmins to bury or bury the poem my father had written and left inside it. Canada had factored so much into his diaries and was the one place he seemed happiest. I ended up instead donating the book to the local Value Village and bringing the poem home, as the book was stultifying (and very dated), and I doubt my father ever read it himself. But through a chain of accidental events, I did end up meeting a new friend and fan, Christina, who introduced me to the owner of Altered Reality, when I realized that all my books would not fit onto the plane home. I was glad to give them to the owner the day before I left, and he requested I sign them. While sitting at his counter signing, my eyes glanced over at a nearby display, where a bunch of crystals in many colors hung sparkling. Seeing them, everything came full circle for me, and I burst out crying, to my mortification. Several minutes passed before I could get myself under control enough to talk, and when I did, I babbled something about being alone in a strange country. Both of them were very understanding, while I got myself together. Before I left, I purchased one of the crystals with the last of my Canadian money from my father's house, feeling a last bit of anger and angst leave me as I left the store. When I returned home, I hung it in the window, and tucked away the poem with the other writings of my father.

I think of my father when I watch certain movies or series he liked, such as Ghost Rider, The Shield, Prison Break, or Star Wars. Watching Independence Day this past summer, I found myself in tears at the moment the alkie father gives his life to save his children (and the rest of the world). I can't help wishing that my father got to go out like that, saving the world or something equally momentous to him in a blaze of glory, instead of passing from the world with the soft wheeze of slow suffocation, unable to save himself.

I still have not driven by my father's house, though I'm sure all this time later that the new owner is all done with his work, and for the first time in my lifetime, the structure has all its walls, working electricity, working plumbing, a habitable basement, and a yard that can be mowed and safely walked through. I still am reminded time to time of how it looked in there, and I tell myself each time that I did the best I could, trying to make sense of the mess, and make sure that what was salvageable went to people who could use it. I always wish that I could have found a way to salvage more. Slowly the many items I took—hot-air balloon towels, clothes, garage door lube, matches, T-shirts—are being used up. Some, like the collection of Cathy cartoons that I've nearly memorized from multiple readings, have become a part of my daily routine. Others will last me the rest of my life, as will the two patchwork quilts I made out of the many stained and slightly chewed Blue Moon sweatshirts found in his attic (the ones I found that were whole/unstained I took to the family reunion that summer after he passed, the remaining few left after that I sent to the woman who bought the Blue Moon). I find that comforting, too. Seeing the house transformed will also be a healing step, its just one I'm not ready to take yet. I think that's because it's the last step of letting go.

The older you get, the less things stay the same. Stores close, and new ones open, buildings are razed, streets are widened, and trees grow and die and are toppled in storms. As horrible as the house was, it was one place that for me never changed, a constant in my world from the time I was little. I'm very grateful that its finally becoming the home it was meant to be, and I hope that with a new family it will lose its ever-present sadness. But it will also no longer be my father's house. Even in the days we weren't speaking, I'd sometimes drive past when life took me to that part of town, and know that my father was there living his life, his broken down truck in the driveway, the porch listing and overflowing with odds and ends, the place I often left him cookies on his birthday in later years with his card. Food was one gift I'm glad to say he always both appreciated and used.

We build our lives from what our parents give us, and what we can glean from the world. Sometimes we build foolishly, and we're not even half finished when the castle comes toppling down. Other times we are almost set to put the crowning last touch on our perfect, solid creation, when a disaster not under our control smashes everything to pieces. Cleaning a spot in the rubble is hard, and so is salvage work, sifting through dreams and having to let some go that are too damaged to ever fly again. Giving up pieces of yourself is probably the hardest thing we ever do, but its how we grow as humans to become more than we are. You have to keep the best, and leave the rest. Then we grit our teeth and start to build again.

***

I published this book before the true ending was ready. The work was both a process of grief and healing and also a result as well; as such, I needed to write and publish it to work through my feelings about my father. But real healing and the grieving process take time, not just understanding. In short, I felt relief and much lighter the moment the book went live on Amazon…while feeling also that the ending, while all I could emotionally manage at the time, was insufficient for the work, and what I was trying to say overall. When something has been part of your life for your whole life it is hard to let go of, even if holding on to it causes you harm. Once you let go, that chapter of your life is truly closed. This feeling of incompleteness in WMFNTM has only grown with the years since the book was published.

My avoidance of my father's former house is that last step for me of healing…and how the book should have concluded. And these years later, I have still not visited that house. For as good as it will be to see someone else has made a true home of the property, it also means acceptance that my father is not there anymore. He will never get a chance to come to his senses and rebuild a relationship with me or make all those dreams of his life into reality. His life, while adventurous and exciting, ended with a lot of failure because he didn't learn from his mistakes, or even admit some decisions were mistakes. The crux of adult life is not only admitting and fixing what mistakes we make, but also learning from problems to mitigate future ones. It is looking without blinders at the sum of our lives on a regular basis and making real lasting changes if we don't like what we see.

How does a person want to be remembered? I think my father would be proud that he had a book written about him (even though I can see him giving me a reproachful look as he grumpily asks why I couldn't have left out some of the more sordid bits). My short answer would be that "To tell your story, Dad, I needed to show the whole man, not the edited version." I don't think anyone reading the book would see him as anything but human. He was both hero and villain, a good friend and brother, and a sometimes-good father.

Made in the USA
Monee, IL
14 May 2024

58437110R10059